BEING HURT AND HURTING OTHERS: CHILDREN'S NARRATIVE ACCOUNTS AND MORAL JUDGMENTS OF THEIR OWN INTERPERSONAL CONFLICTS

Cecilia Wainryb
Beverly A. Brehl
Sonia Matwin

WITH COMMENTARY BY
Bryan W. Sokol
Stuart Hammond

Willis F. Overton
Series Editor

MONOGRAPHS OF THE SOCIETY FOR RESEARCH IN CHILD DEVELOPMENT

Serial No. 281, Vol. 70, No. 3, 2005

 **Blackwell** Publishing *Boston, Massachusetts   Oxford, United Kingdom*

BEING HURT AND HURTING OTHERS: CHILDREN'S NARRATIVE ACCOUNTS AND MORAL JUDGMENTS OF THEIR OWN INTERPERSONAL CONFLICTS

CONTENTS

COMMENTARY

ABSTRACT

Children's narrative accounts and moral evaluations of their own interpersonal conflicts with peers were examined. Girls and boys ($N = 112$) in preschool ($M = 4.8$ years), first grade ($M = 6.9$ years), fifth grade ($M = 10.9$ years), and tenth grade ($M = 16.2$ years) provided one narrative of a time when they had been hurt by a peer ("victim"), and one of a time when they had hurt a peer ("perpetrator"). Victim and perpetrator narratives were equally long and detailed and depicted similar types of harmful behaviors, but differed significantly in terms of various measures of content and coherence. Narratives given from the victim's perspective featured a self-referential focus and a fairly coherent structure. When the same children gave accounts of situations in which they had been the perpetrators, their construals were less coherent and included multiple shifts between references to their own experience and the experience of the other. Children's moral judgments also varied by perspective, with the majority of victims making negative judgments and nearly half the perpetrators making positive or mixed judgments. These differences in moral judgments were related to the distinct ways in which victims and perpetrators construed conflict situations. Age differences were also found in both narrative construals and moral evaluations, but regardless of their age children construed conflict situations differently from the victim's and the perpetrator's perspectives. By integrating, within the study of moral development, children's interpretations of the social interactions that are at the basis of moral thinking, this approach brings us a step closer to conceptualizing the study of children's moral behavior.

I. MORALITY, INTERPRETATION, AND PERSPECTIVE

STATEMENT OF THE PROBLEM

The question of how children's moral judgments relate to their moral behavior is central to the study of moral development, not because all that really matters is what children do, but because knowing only children's judgments of right and wrong is insufficient for understanding their moral lives. Moral development research conducted over the last 25 years has demonstrated that, in contrast to what was previously assumed (Kohlberg, 1969, 1971), even young children reason that it is wrong to hurt or mistreat others not because there are rules against it but because of the moral concern with the welfare of others (for reviews of this research, see Helwig & Turiel, 2002; Smetana, 2006; Tisak, 1995; Turiel, 1998). And yet, children do hurt others, and are often hurt by others. The concrete instances in which this happens hold in them an inherent tension between what children think and what they sometimes do. How do children grasp these situations? What sense do they make of them? What do they think about themselves and others and whatever circumstances lead up to such hurtful interactions?

Over the years, assessments of the consistency between moral judgments and moral behavior have yielded inconclusive data, with findings pointing to some realms of consistency as well as variations and inconsistencies (e.g., Blasi, 1980, 1993; Derryberry & Thoma, 2005). The limited success of this approach has been due, at least in part, to the framing of the question as one of consistency between moral judgments made in the abstract and moral behaviors in specific contexts (see also Turiel, 1990, 2003). The research reported in this *Monograph* does not directly examine the relation between moral thought and moral action. Such an endeavor is premature, as to adequately address such questions it is necessary to first understand how children apply their moral concepts, along with other types of concepts, to real and concrete interpersonal contexts. *This* is the topic of this *Monograph*.

The typical strategy of moral development research has been to assess children's moral reasoning about hypothetical situations (for comprehensive reviews, see Helwig & Turiel, 2002; Smetana, 2006; Tisak, 1995; Turiel,

1998). Whereas there have also been studies assessing children's (and adults') reasoning about real conflict situations (e.g., Krebs, Denton, & Wark, 2002; Smetana, Schlagman, & Adams, 1993; Smetana et al., 1999; Turiel, 2005; Walker, de Vries, & Trevethan, 1987; Walker, Pitts, Hennig, & Matsuba, 1999; Wark & Krebs, 1996), their focus has largely been on comparing the moral judgments and justifications that children make about real conflicts with those they make about hypothetical conflicts. None of these approaches can fully capture how children make sense of those situations in which they actually hurt someone or someone hurts them. To understand how children think about situations of interpersonal conflict in which they were directly involved requires integrating, within the study of moral development, a seldom considered aspect of children's thinking, namely, their construals of their conflicting interactions. How do children interpret—what is it that they pay attention to, how do they understand—those interpersonal interactions in which they themselves either hurt or are hurt by another person?

In the course of social interactions in which one person is mistreated or hurt by another, children routinely notice certain features of the interactions and attach to those features certain meanings. Other children observing or involved in the same situations may notice other features, or may attach to the same features different meanings. Understanding children's specific construals of an interaction is thus important because, ultimately, children will end up making moral judgments about whatever understandings they formed of those aspects of the situation that happened to be salient to them (Wainryb, 2000, 2004). Perhaps less apparent, but nonetheless central to our view, is that these moments are the raw materials of which moral development is made up—children develop moral understandings by reflecting on their subjective construals of the features of social interactions (Nucci, 2004a; Turiel, 1983, 1998).

What further complicates this process is that, by definition, moral conflicts involve two distinct perspectives—the perpetrator's and the victim's. We expect that children experience and construe conflict situations differently depending on their specific perspective, which is not to say that children are incapable of understanding (or unwilling, or even unlikely to understand) another child's point of view, or of looking at events from another child's perspective. Our argument, rather, is that when children are in the position of being, say, punched or excluded, they are likely to attend to and make sense of aspects of the goings-on quite differently than when they are the ones punching or excluding someone else.

Research documenting the nature of the conflicts spontaneously arising among children (Shantz, 1987; Shantz & Hartup, 1992) has provided important information about the general parameters (who–when–what) of these conflicts, but much less is known regarding the meanings that these

2

conflicts may have for the children involved in them. Whereas research has shown that children consider multiple aspects of conflict situations in which they had been directly involved, such as goals, emotions, contextual factors, and outcomes (e.g., Murphy & Eisenberg, 2002; Shantz, 1993), there is no evidence for whether those features are differentially understood by victims and perpetrators. Similarly, whereas research has shown that victims and perpetrators tend to make different judgments of hypothetical and real transgressions (e.g., Dunn, Cutting, & Demetriou, 2000; Krebs et al., 2002; Smetana et al., 1999), there is no evidence linking children's different moral judgments to distinct construals of social interactions.

As shall become more apparent once we delve into the details of this research, the task of capturing children's construals from different perspectives is not straightforward as it requires finding ways to extract, from children's descriptions of their interactions, detailed information about what Bruner (1986) has aptly termed the "landscape of action" and the "landscape of consciousness." Concretely, this means using multiple formal assessments to record children's references to what, in their view, happened in a particular situation, who engaged in precisely which harmful behavior, what circumstances preceded and surrounded the event, and what consequences ensued, as well as the sorts of intentions, thoughts, and feelings that children attribute to themselves and to the child with whom they were in conflict. We have included in this *Monograph* detailed explanations and examples of the procedures we have used to accomplish this task.

Much can be learned from examining the very specific and concrete ways in which children construe their social interactions, that is of value for understanding their moral lives. By systematically examining children's construals of moral situations, this research brings to the fore the role of interpretation in moral thinking. By moving beyond the assessment of moral judgments made from an uninvolved third-person perspective, it underscores the possibility that children apply their moral concepts differently when they judge instances of harm or injustice from the victim's or the perpetrator's perspectives. Together, these issues are important as they ultimately bear on how children's moral concepts both fit and develop within their actual social interactions, especially those interactions that appear to violate those very moral concepts. By contributing to our understanding of children's moral thinking as it is manifested in their everyday interactions, this research also brings us a step closer to better conceptualizing the study of children's moral behavior.

This approach also has implications for the study of moral development. Whereas the evidence (e.g., Helwig & Turiel, 2002; Smetana, 2006) indicating that children judge it wrong to hurt or mistreat others regardless of their age is compelling, it should not be taken to mean that children's experiences with moral transgressions, and their understandings of those experiences, do not change with age. The study of children's construals and interpretations of those situations is likely to shed light on the nature of age differences in moral experiences. Given the evidence that, with age, children become more adept at taking the perspective of others (Flavell, 1968; Flavell, Green, & Flavell, 1986; Gurucharri & Selman, 1982; Selman, 1980, 1994) and understanding others' minds (Astington, Harris, & Olson, 1988; Harris, 1989, 1991; Lalonde & Chandler, 2002; Wellman, 2002), it would not be surprising to find that younger and older children (this study includes children between the ages of 5 and 16) interpret situations of interpersonal conflict in substantially different ways. Because interpretations and moral judgments are likely to be closely intertwined, the challenge will be to make sense of what, precisely, develops.

Finally, and more generally, this approach aims to show that it is both possible and necessary to fully integrate within the study of moral development a concern for the subjectivity and specificity of children's actual social and moral interactions, while at the same time not only eschewing moral relativism but highlighting the prescriptive nature of children's moral thinking as it gets played out—regrets, justifications, doubts, and all—in their actual moral lives. In this regard, our work draws on a broad and longstanding intellectual enterprise, initiated by Turiel (1983, 1998, 2002) and elaborated by many others (Helwig, 2006; Horn, 2005; Kahn, 2006; Killen, Lee-Kim, McGlothlin, & Stangor, 2002; Laupa, 2000; Neff & Helwig, 2002; Nucci, 2001, 2002; Smetana, 1999, 2006; Tisak, Tisak, & Goldstein, 2006) that brings moral, epistemic, and constructivist concerns to bear jointly on the study of how children actively develop a domain of moral concerns in the context of their social interactions. It is only in the context of the wealth of evidence concerning children's prescriptive moral judgments that our propositions and findings can be fully understood. And so, before we describe our research and interpret our detailed findings, we turn to chart the path we have taken from prescriptivity to subjectivity and, hopefully, back.

THE STUDY OF CHILDREN'S MORAL JUDGMENTS

Over the last 25 years moral development researchers, working from what has come to be known as the "domain-specific" tradition (Turiel, 1983, 1998), have altered the way we understand children's morality by demonstrating that even young children (as young as 3) judge it to be wrong and unacceptable to hurt or mistreat others, not merely because of the potential for ensuing punishment but rather because of their concerns with fairness and the well-being of persons. The results of more than 100 studies

4

comparing children's thinking about matters bearing on harm and injustice and matters bearing on social convention have indicated that from early ages on, children draw distinctions between the two domains of social life (Helwig & Turiel, 2002; Smetana, 2006; Turiel, 1983, 1998). Whereas children are rule oriented when evaluating social conventional transgressions, they focus on the consequences of acts for others when evaluating moral transgressions, and evaluate straightforward moral transgressions as being wrong regardless of rules or custom. Children's moral understandings have been shown to develop from a focus on concrete harm in early childhood, to an understanding of fairness defined in terms of equality and equal treatment between persons in middle childhood (Damon, 1977; Davidson, Turiel, & Black, 1983; Smetana, 2006). Research has also shown that children bring to bear their moral concepts on straightforward instances of physical harm (e.g., hitting or kicking), psychological harm (e.g., teasing, calling a child names), and unfairness (e.g., failing to share or take turns), as well as on multifaceted situations that entail overlapping concerns with morality, social conventions, and personal choice (e.g., Helwig, 2006; Killen et al., 2002; Smetana, Killen, & Turiel, 1991).

Most of the evidence on children's moral thinking comes from assessments of children's evaluations of hypothetical moral transgressions. The reliance on assessments of judgments unencumbered by considerations likely to have arisen if children had been asked to judge conflicts in which they were directly involved has enabled researchers to assess children's moral competence. But how do these findings bear on children's reasoning about their own conflicts with others? In a number of studies (Smetana et al., 1993, 1999; Turiel, 2005) children's reasoning about hypothetical moral transgressions was compared with their reasoning about actual transgressions that had been observed in classrooms or playgrounds at their schools. Findings indicated that, whether judging hypothetical or actual conflicts, children distinguished moral from conventional transgressions and made negative judgments of all transgressions (hypothetical and actual) entailing unfairness or harm to others. These findings suggested that assessments of moral reasoning in the context of hypothetical situations *are* relevant to the understanding of how children reason in regard to actual, real-life conflicts.

Nevertheless, comparisons between judgments about hypothetical and actual conflicts also revealed a number of differences. In general, children had more difficulties explaining why the actual transgressions were wrong, and their judgments about those events were less prescriptive and generalizable than their judgments about the hypothetical events. A similar pattern of findings has been reported by researchers comparing (largely among adolescents and adults) reasoning about hypothetical and real-life dilemmas from the perspective of moral stages rather than domains. Their findings, too, indicated that although levels of moral reasoning are fairly

5

consistent across both types of dilemmas (Walker et al., 1987, 1999), real-life conflicts tend to feature slightly lower stage judgments than hypothetical dilemmas (for reviews see, Krebs, Vermeulen, Carpendale, & Denton, 1991; Krebs et al., 2002).

These differences are not surprising given that several features of importance distinguish hypothetical from actual conflict situations. In research stimuli depicting hypothetical conflicts, such as those used in moral development research, the relevant features of situations are deliberately crafted and, often, spelled out (e.g., "Tommy pushed Amy off the swing on purpose, as hard as he could, and made her cry"). Outside the confines of research laboratories, the features of conflict situations—features upon which evaluations ultimately depend, such as whether or not Tommy, for example, pushed Amy on purpose—are not spelled out. The characters' beliefs, intentions, and goals do not appear as subtitles, and thus are often difficult to discern and fleeting. In constructing their understandings of actual conflict situations, children may or may not attend to Tommy's intention, and if they do, they may or may not interpret Tommy's behavior as having been "on purpose." Furthermore, intentions are not the sole relevant feature; interpersonal situations are constituted by myriad features, including children's relationship history, emotions, and thoughts, just to name a few (Murphy & Eisenberg, 2002; Shantz, 1993). In making sense of actual interpersonal situations, children are likely to attend to some of those features and not others and are bound, moreover, to form their own understandings of whichever features they view as salient or relevant. Also, whereas hypothetical conflicts commonly refer to discrete social encounters, children tend to understand and negotiate their actual conflicts over the course of a series of encounters and in light of their interpretation of their ongoing relationships.

Another distinctive characteristic of hypothetical stimuli is that they generally place those making the judgments (i.e., the research participants) in an outsider's or observer's perspective. Typically, however, children directly engaged in conflicts are not in the position of observers. Instead, they are much more likely to be either in the position of the "victim" or in the position of the "perpetrator," shift positions during the course of a conflict, or even disagree with one another as to which position each occupied. Indeed, research conducted in preschools (Smetana et al., 1993, 1999) and elementary and secondary schools (e.g., Sedlak & Walton, 1982; Turiel, 2005; Walton, 1985) confirms that children can be readily observed in each of these roles.

Given the distinct features of hypothetical and actual moral conflict situations, it bears asking how researchers interested in studying children's thinking about actual moral conflicts should proceed. Several years ago Walker and colleagues, concerned with the limited usefulness of hypothetical dilemmas for understanding "how people ordinarily conceptualize the moral domain and interpret moral problems" (Walker et al., 1999, p. 376), proceeded to conduct a fairly large-scale study in which participants (ages 16–84) were asked to describe examples of moral dilemmas they had experienced as well as examples of what they considered to be difficult moral conflicts. These data were analyzed for content and stage, largely in terms of themes in Kohlberg's stages. The one striking finding to emerge, beyond the expected differences in moral stages and moral orientations, concerned the many specific and highly contextualized references (e.g., to practical considerations, nuances of relationships, religious duties) featured in participants' descriptions of their dilemmas—references that, in the view of Walker and colleagues, could not be captured using such a coding system. Reinforced, at least in part, by these findings, Walker concluded that contemporary moral psychology cannot adequately capture moral maturity and turned, in subsequent research, to assess notions of religion, spirituality, and moral excellence (Walker, 2004; Walker & Pitts, 1998).

It may well be that Walker was right in arguing that the notions of religion and spirituality merit more attention within the study of moral development, but that is beyond the point as far as our discussion goes. Furthermore, Walker may or may not have been right in concluding that Kohlberg's theory is limited (we do, however, contest the implication that Kohlberg's theory represents all of contemporary moral psychology), but this is also beyond the point. Our point is that Walker's is not the only (or even the main) conclusion to be drawn from the aforementioned data. For it appears that it was not participants' moral judgments that could not be captured by the stage system, but their specific framing of the dilemmas they faced. What was missing, we speculate, was a systematic consideration of the ways in which participants construed those situations. Missing also from this approach was the recognition that moral conflicts typically include someone who is being victimized—who is likely to experience and construe the events bearing on his or her victimization differently from whoever is causing such harm.

There is a sense in which we do agree with Walker and colleagues, for we too think that current approaches to the study of moral development cannot fully capture the complexities of children's thinking about conflict situations in which they had been directly involved. We do think, however, that it is possible to address these issues within existing formulations of moral development (though perhaps not Kohlberg's). It is our view that for the purpose of addressing these issues it is necessary to integrate, within the scope of moral development research, the construals that children make of conflict situations from different perspectives. In subsequent sections we consider research findings that bear on the potential roles of construal and perspective in moral development, thereby providing a more fully fleshed-out rationale for the investigation of children's construals of conflict situations in which they had been involved as victims or perpetrators.

THE CONSTRUAL OF MORAL TRANSGRESSIONS

The notions of subjective construal or interpretation—the idea that persons construe their own reality—are inextricably associated (or so it would seem) with social constructionist and postmodern thought (Gergen, 1991; Rosenau, 1992; Shweder, 1999). Within such a view, however, the rejection of objectivism is accompanied by a wholesale rejection of deep structures, directionality, and integration. This is by no means the only worldview within which the notions of construal and interpretation can comfortably rest. Over 50 years ago, Gestalt psychologists hoisted the "subjectivist banner" (Griffin, Dunning, & Ross, 1990; Ross & Nisbett, 1991; Ross & Ward, 1996) and put forth what at the time was the revolutionary proposition that interpretive activity is fundamental to knowing. In stark opposition to behaviorist claims about stimulus–response associations, research by Gestalt psychologists provided ample empirical evidence that "objects of judgment" (i.e., whatever one makes judgments about) are not fixed and do not reside in the events themselves. Instead, objects of judgment are cognitively created and transformed as individuals interpret unfolding events (Asch, 1952; Duncker, 1939). Gestalt psychology was not alone in its attack of behaviorism. At about the same time, Piaget's (1952, 1971; Piaget & Inhelder, 1969) seminal ideas and research gave impetus to a long-standing tradition in developmental psychology that, departing from behaviorist assumptions, views children, and persons in general, as actively construing, rather than passively registering, reality. In sharp contrast to the radical subjectivism underlying social constructionist and postmodern views, views such as those espoused by Asch and Piaget, and by contemporary psychologists working from those traditions (e.g., Chandler, 1993; Langer, 1994; Nisbett, 2005; Overton, 2004; Ross, 1990; Turiel, 2002), predicate that knowledge is the product of the interaction between persons and their independently structured environments. In Piaget's (2000, p. 35) words, "Knowledge, at its origin, neither arises from objects nor from the subject, but from interactions—at first inextricable—between the subject and those objects."

Whereas the proposition that persons construe their own reality spurred an interest among psychologists working in fields as diverse as aggression (e.g., Dodge, 1986, 2003), depression (e.g., Beck, 1967; Dalgleish et al., 2003), peer relations (e.g., Asher & Wheeler, 1985; Crick & Ladd, 1993; Prinstein, Cheah, & Guyer, 2005), everyday problem solving (e.g., Berg, Meegan, & Deviney, 1998), and emotional development (e.g., Lewis, 2001; Weiner & Graham, 1985), this has not been the case in the field of moral development. Although it is hard to say with certainty why, we speculate that this may have been due, at least in part, to the ever-present concern that attending to the subjective ways in which individuals interpret moral conflicts would inevitably lead to moral relativism.

It was Kohlberg (1971) who first issued the injunction against confounding matters of value ("ought") with matters of fact ("is"), and it is important to acknowledge that, in so doing, Kohlberg successfully steered the field of moral psychology away from the tautological and relativistic definitions of morality offered by behaviorist psychology. Indeed, the considerable advances in moral psychology over the past several decades rest, to a large extent, on Kohlberg's clarity of vision and continued and emphatic argument against the relativistic tendency to determine "how things ought to be" on the basis of "how things are."

Nevertheless, it is also important to recognize that allowing for the possibility that children, and people in general, subjectively construe moral situations does not necessarily lead to moral relativism. This, however, was not clear in Kohlberg's stage theory of moral development. Kohlberg (1969, 1971) viewed moral development as an increasing process of differentiation, by which moral understandings come to be distinguished from prudential and conventional understandings. In this view, moral thinking at the early stages is contingent on self-serving concerns and existing rules because, in the thinking of young children, "is" and "ought" are not yet distinguished, and it is only with development that matters of "ought" become extricated from the "is" and moral judgments become "entirely independent of factual assumptions" (Kohlberg, 1971, p. 292) and thus generalizable and universal. Kohlberg's emphasis on the increasing differentiation between matters of is and ought worked to obscure the possibility that beliefs and interpretations concerning the ways things are may play a role in moral thinking after moral concepts have become prescriptive (Wainryb, 2004). A different developmental framework—one that does not rely on moral concepts stemming from nonmoral concepts—renders this possibility less problematic.

In the constructivist and interactional view of moral development put forth by Turiel (1983, 1998), for example, children construct prescriptive moral concepts, not by distinguishing them from nonmoral concepts, but out of their social interactions. That is, children's perceptions and interpretations of the features of those interactions (e.g., their construal of the consequences of an insult or a violation of a promise) constitute the basis upon which children develop prescriptive moral concepts. This is not to say that children decide what is right or wrong based on how things are. What it does say is that children's beliefs about the ways things are—their

9

interpretations of what actually happens—serve as a background against which moral judgments are made (Wainryb, 2000, 2004). This proposition makes room for variation and subjectivity in moral judgments, but associates the variation and subjectivity not with relativism at the level of moral concepts, but with relativism at the level of understandings (or construals) of reality—a crucial difference aptly described by Asch (1952) as the difference between moral relativism and "relational determination of meanings" (see also Duncker, 1939; Turiel, Killen, & Helwig, 1987; Wainryb, 1991, 2004).

That persons make moral judgments in relation to their own interpretations or understandings of the relevant facts is plainly evident in the nature of the controversies surrounding complex social issues, such as abortion, pornography, or capital punishment. The variability in opinions about these matters, as expressed in public discourse as well as in legal opinions, clearly revolves around ambiguities in basic assumptions and construals of the features of those acts. As examples, the definition of life and the determination of its beginning are ambiguous concepts that are difficult to specify. The consequences of pornography are also in dispute, with some believing that it leads to violent and criminal behavior and others disputing such a causal connection. The deterring potential of capital punishment has been an equally disputed subject. The ambivalence concerning these assumptions exists not only in the thinking of experts in the relevant disciplines but also in the thinking of the lay person, and research with adolescents and adults has shown that their positive or negative evaluations of those issues were systematically associated with their differing beliefs or construals about the relevant "facts" (Turiel, Hildebrandt, & Wainryb, 1991).

This phenomenon—that people make moral judgments in relation to their specific construals of the relevant facts—is not restricted to larger societal issues or to the reasoning of adolescents and adults. Like adolescents and adults, children continuously appraise the features of the social contexts in which they participate, and make judgments that vary systematically with their own construals and interpretations of those contexts. Children, even young children, may differently construe ordinary events in their social lives, such as conflicts over turn-taking, teasing, name-calling, or exclusion. Children may differently construe the relevant facts (e.g., whether Frank did or did not have his turn at the swing already; whether or not tossing Lisa's hat around the room was part of the game). They may also differently construe what others believe (e.g., did she, or did she not, really believe that calling her son "lazy" would motivate him to work harder?), or intended to do (e.g., did Dylan want to hurt Carl's feelings by ignoring him, or was he merely preoccupied with other issues?). Children might also construct different understandings of a situation because they differentially attend to various aspects of the situation.

10

Although the possibility that children make moral judgments in relation to their specific interpretation of situations was considered by Asch (1952; see also Duncker, 1939; Hatch, 1983) many years ago and subsequently discussed in the context of empirical findings (e.g., Berndt & Berndt, 1975; Sedlak, 1979), it did not receive systematic consideration until more recently. In the 1990s we began systematically documenting aspects of the interpretive process that go into making moral judgments. Because a child's construal of a moral situation involves multiple elements concerning the landscapes of "action" (e.g., who did what, how, when) and "consciousness" (e.g., what was he thinking, feeling, wanting; what was I thinking, feeling, wanting), we began with a simple heuristic. In an effort to demonstrate, first, that children make moral judgments in reference to whatever they understand or believe to be true about an event, we manipulated what participants believed to be true about a particular issue and assessed whether their moral judgments varied according to the new beliefs.

In one study, for example, participants were asked to discuss corporal punishment, and spontaneously referred to their own understandings of the actual consequences of corporal punishment (Wainryb, 1991). Their beliefs in this regard were not uniform; some believed that corporal punishment functions in ways that actually do help young children to learn and remember, whereas others believed that corporal punishment does not have such positive (and has some negative) consequences. Their moral judgments (obtained separately) were, unsurprisingly, associated with what they held to be true, such that participants who construed corporal punishment as having positive consequences judged it more positively than those who viewed it as lacking such consequences. Participants were then asked to entertain the possibility of new information that "proved" their original information to be inaccurate and the opposite information to be true. Under this experimental manipulation, in which participants agreed as a matter of fact to a different construal of the consequences of corporal punishment, the majority of participants changed their moral judgments in accordance with the new information (though fewer did so among those who originally held that corporal punishment was wrong). Subsequent research has shown that the relation between factual understandings and moral judgments can be observed in children's thinking about a broad range of moral practices entailing concerns with injustice, psychological harm, and even physical harm. For example, children as young as 5 (but not younger; Wainryb & Ford, 1998) recognized that the moral evaluation of practices such as preventing girls from attending school (Wainryb, Shaw, & Maianu, 1998), calling children "dumb" to help them learn (Wainryb & Ford, 1998), and beating misbehaving children with sticks (Shaw & Wainryb, 1999; Wainryb 1993) depends on what one believes to be true about aspects relevant to each situation.

Even as this body of research did not comprehensively assess children's construals of reality but focused, heuristically, on children's factual beliefs, it nevertheless provided systematic support for the proposition that, throughout development, children apply prescriptive (i.e., nonrelative) moral concepts against the background of their own varied understandings of reality. These findings also demonstrated that variation in moral judgments can be distinguished from and examined in reference to variations in the ways reality is understood or construed. This, in turn, has allowed us to acknowledge the variation and subjectivity in children's (and adults') moral judgments while at the same time eschewing a position of moral relativism.

And yet, because the main purpose of this body of research was to establish that a relation exists, across development, between children's beliefs about reality and their moral thinking, the methods used consisted of assessing children's judgments in relation to specific factual beliefs that were explicitly given and manipulated in hypothetical research stimuli. This methodology was not meant to (and did not) assess how children go about construing reality. Clues as to the features that children may include in their construals of social interactions come from moral development research and from research on children's conflicts.

Moral development research has underscored the importance of intentions and emotions. Piaget's (1932) early observations of young children's constrained understandings of intentions in the context of their moral thinking were followed by research suggesting that as long as information about intentions is given explicitly and is not confounded with information about consequences, even 5- and 6-year-olds judge intentional acts to be more wrong than accidental acts (Berndt & Berndt, 1975; Darley & Zanna, 1982; Karniol, 1978; Keasey, 1977; Nelson-Le Gall, 1985; Shultz, Wright, & Schleifer, 1986). If children are not asked to weigh intentions against consequences, even 3-year-olds can distinguish between a deliberate and an accidental breach (Harris & Nunez, 1996; Nunez & Harris, 1998; Siegel & Peterson, 1998). Research has also shown that children's understandings (and misunderstandings) of emotions are central to their moral judgments (Arsenio & Lover, 1999; Arsenio, Gold, & Adams, 2006; Denham & Kochanoff, 2002; Dunn, 1999, 2006; Harris, 1989; Turiel, 1998), and that even toddlers use their basic understandings of other people's emotions to comfort, tease, and hurt others (e.g., Dunn, 1999, 2006; Dunn & Slomkowski, 1992) and to identify situations in which rules are violated (e.g., Denham & Kochanoff, 2002). It has also been suggested that the primitive nature of young children's understandings of intention (e.g., Astington, 2001; Schult, 2002; Wellman, 2002) and emotion (Arsenio et al., 2006; Denham & Kochankoff, 2002; Gnepp & Klayman, 1992; Harris, 1989; Harter & Whitesell, 1989; Keller, Gummerum, Wang, & Lindsey, 2004;

Lagattuta, 2005; Shaw & Wainryb, 2005) constrains their moral thinking in significant ways (Wainryb & Brehl, in press).

Together, this research has shown that, when information about beliefs, intentions, and emotions is explicitly given in hypothetical stimuli, children account for these features in their moral judgments. Less is known about whether children actually consider these features on their own, when they construe their social interactions. A study (Shantz, 1993) in which twenty-seven 7-year-olds were asked to recall an argument or fight they had had with a peer at school does suggest that, even when unprobed, children consider multiple aspects of their interactions, including the nature of the conflict (e.g., physical harm, possession), the history of the relationship with their adversary, as well as their own and the other child's emotions. Interestingly, references to intentions or reasons either were not featured in children's descriptions of their interactions, or not coded. In a more recent study (Murphy & Eisenberg, 2002) including a larger sample of 7- to 11-year-olds, children were directly questioned about their goals and reasons in the course of recent conflicts they had had with peers (e.g., "When _____ happened, what were you trying to do, what did you want to happen?"). Children seemed to have no difficulty reporting on such goals. It is harder to determine, based on the data, *what* children wanted, as goals were scored (and reported) only in terms of their friendliness or hostility. Nevertheless, the few examples provided suggest that children reported on a variety of intentions ranging from "I wanted to hurt him" and "I wanted to annoy him," through "I wanted her to be happy" and "I was trying to make it fair" (Murphy & Eisenberg, 2002, p. 542). Children in this study were similarly asked about the emotions they had experienced during the event and about the outcome of the conflicts. Whereas children's descriptions of their goals and emotions (as well as of the ways in which the conflicts started and ended) were given in response to direct probing, this research, along with Shantz's (1993), suggests that these elements are likely to be part of children's construals of their own interpersonal conflicts.

Children's construals of social interactions have received more sustained attention from researchers investigating the social cognitive processes of aggressive children. In an effort to test propositions regarding possible explanations of the self-perpetuating nature of the behavior of aggressive children, researchers have closely examined how these children construe ambiguous (largely hypothetical, but see Steinberg & Dodge, 1983) social interactions. This research has shown that aggressive children (as compared with nonaggressive children) differ in the type of contextual cues they recall from the situations depicted, and also attribute hostile intentions to others (for reviews of these data, see Coie & Dodge, 1998; Crick & Dodge, 1994; Dodge, 2003). Other research with aggressive and conduct-disordered children has shown that these children tend to construe conflict situations in ways that highlight the experience of the perpetrator and minimize the experience of the victim (Astor, 1994; Nucci & Herman, 1982; Slaby & Guerra, 1988; Tisak et al., 2006). Research with withdrawn, depressed, and victimized youth (for reviews, see Dodge, 1993, 2003; Graham & Juvonen, 2001) has similarly suggested that their construals display biases in their attribution of causality (e.g., internality, globality, stability).

While these data are not directly informative regarding how children in normative samples might interpret their own experiences of interpersonal conflict, an aspect of this research that is particularly informative for our purposes is the reliable finding that children's construals of social interactions are not copies of reality. Whereas the focus of this research has been the distortions specific to the construals of aggressive children (distortions said to originate in individual differences in information processing; Crick & Dodge, 1994), we hold that *all* construals are, by their nature, not exact copies but interpretations of reality. Even as children, even young children, have understandings about diverse elements of social interactions, their construals might emphasize some and ignore others.

In this regard, it is important to underscore that all construals are made from a specific point of view or perspective. Recall that the purpose of the research we have described early in this section (e.g., Wainryb, 1991, 1993; Wainryb & Ford, 1998; Wainryb et al., 1998) was not to document children's construals of reality, but to ascertain whether their moral judgments were related to specific construals and varied in accordance with those construals. It would thus be a mistake to conclude, based on that research, that children's construals of conflict situations can be studied independently from the perspectives from which they were made. The notions of construal and perspective, at least as dealt with in our work, do not represent separate variables. To fully understand how children construe interpersonal conflict situations in which they were directly involved, it is essential that we attend to the distinct perspectives from which they made those construals. "It is only from a point of view that we represent reality," argued Searle (1995, p. 176), echoing arguments made by Asch (1952) 40 years earlier. We develop this argument in the next section.

THE ROLE OF PERSPECTIVE IN MORAL THINKING

In the context of developmental theory, the proposition that a child's construal of reality depends on her or his perspective is most readily associated with egocentrism and its more developmentally advanced counterpart, perspective-taking (Piaget, 1952, 1954, 1960). The notion of egocentrism received much attention in the late 1950s and through the

1970s, as developmental psychologists concerned themselves with the decline of egocentrism and the gradual development of role-taking, or perspective-taking, skills (Chandler & Helm, 1984; Feffer & Gourevitch, 1960; Flavell, 1968; see also Chandler, 2001). The most comprehensive, and perhaps best-known model of such development was formulated by Selman (1980, 1994; Selman & Byrne, 1974), who conceptualized the changes in perspective-taking abilities in terms of structures or stages. Selman suggested that prior to the age of 6 children are egocentric, in the sense that they make no distinction between their own views and other possible views. With age, children develop an understanding that there are different subjective perspectives, and by adolescence they are capable of taking an "objective" third-person perspective.

Given the posited developmental progression from egocentrism to perspective taking, one might expect that older children would be increasingly less constrained by their own perspective and more able to take a "third-person" perspective on, among other things, interpersonal conflicts. Accordingly, the expectation would be that the role of children's own perspective in their interpretations and evaluations of moral conflicts should systematically decline with age. We have a different understanding of egocentrism, one that captures both the constructive and distortive aspects of the process by which persons come to know and understand reality (Wainryb, 1984). Thus, we also have a different expectation regarding the nature and developmental trajectory of biases associated with one's perspective.

One of the central themes in Piaget's work (Piaget, 1952; Piaget & Inhelder, 1969) has been that individuals, including children and even infants, do not passively register reality but rather actively construe it—interpret it, assimilate it—based on what they know and what they perceive as given. This proposition has two parts. One part (discussed in the previous section) is that individuals actively construct their understandings of reality. The other is that, in doing so, they define reality according to their own perspective. Even as he acknowledged that the term "egocentrism" was problematic, Piaget (1962/2000) also underscored the rationale that guided him in choosing it: "I have used the term egocentrism to designate the initial inability to decenter, to shift the given cognitive perspective. It might have been better to say simply 'centrism,' but since the initial centering is always relative to one's own position and action, I said 'egocentrism' . . ." (p. 243).

Children, and people in general, experience their own actions, feelings, and ideas more directly than those of others. Piaget (1970) alluded to this in talking about "the primacy of the subject's own action and point of view, the only action and point of view he knows at first" (p. 3). What this means, we think, is that even though older children are likely to be more capable of

15

entertaining alternative points of view than are their younger peers, they too are bound to find it difficult, or at the very least effortful, to suppress their own viewpoints. Unavoidably, and regardless of age, children's own actions, feelings, and ideas will serve as the filter through which the experiences of others are understood. Therefore, our expectation is that children's perspectives on interpersonal conflicts—their position as victim or perpetrator—will color their understandings and interpretations of those situations, regardless of their age.

The idea that one's perspective makes a difference to how one construes reality—including moral realities—has also been invoked within discursive approaches to psychology (Bamberg, 1997, 2004; Davies & Harré, 1990; Harré & Moghaddam, 2003; Harré & van Langenhove, 1991). In this approach, however, the notion of "positioning" is typically associated with an emphasis on emergent processes and the (implicit) dismissal of developmental processes (Korobov & Bamberg, 2004). We take a more "robust" view (some might characterize our view as "modern," as compared with "postmodern"; Chandler, 1993) of development. Thus, to distinguish between positioning theory and our own propositions regarding the "perspectival" nature of construal, we speak about perspectives rather than positions.

Evidence in support of the proposition that the perspective from which one interprets a situation matters comes from many quarters. A compelling body of evidence comes from attribution research. The central question of classic attribution theory has been how people explain social behavior (Heider, 1958), and one of its central findings is that adults' explanations of social behavior feature systematic biases, with people explaining their own behavior by appealing to situational factors and the behaviors of others by appealing to traits and dispositional factors (Jones & Nisbett, 1987; for comprehensive reviews of research, see Malle, 2004; Pronin, Gilovich, & Ross, 2004; Ross & Nisbett, 1991). More recently, research has shown that people also attribute to others, but not to themselves, cognitive and emotional biases and nonnormative beliefs, values, and priorities (Pronin et al., 2004; see also Ehrlinger, Gilovich, & Ross, 2005; Ross & Ward, 1996). Other research (e.g., Malle & Knobe, 1997; Malle & Pearce, 2001) has shown that when explaining their own behavior people focus on their own mental states and feelings (e.g., "I am hurt"), but when explaining another's behavior the focus is on the other person's actions (e.g., "he yells"). When taken together, findings from attribution research suggest that people's interpretations are heavily colored by their perspective.

In addition to the findings stemming from social psychological research, there are research findings bearing more directly on moral thinking that suggest that people who occupy different positions in society tend to develop different perspectives, and different interpretations, of the same

situations. As an example, research conducted within a hierarchically organized and patriarchal community in the Middle East (Wainryb & Turiel,
1994; see also Turiel & Wainryb, 1994, 2000) has shown that girls and
women, who occupy subordinate positions in society, and men who occupy
dominant positions, reason differently about the meaning and legitimacy of
some of their own cultural practices. In one such case, when discussing
cultural restrictions imposed on women but not on men, female participants
emphasized the serious pragmatic consequences that ensue from violating
those restrictions (e.g., abandonment, physical harm, divorce) and judged
those practices to be unfair, whereas male participants focused more on the
distinct roles of men and women in the family and on the societal harmony
that ensues from respecting (and enforcing) such distinctions.

The phenomenon of distinct evaluations being associated with distinct
social positions is not restricted to other cultures or to relatively rigid and
culturally established power differentials. Findings from a series of studies
with adolescents and their parents in the United States suggest that even
within the context of fairly harmonious relationships, teens and their parents develop distinct interpretations concerning the conflicts they experience in their families with regard to restrictions imposed on the teens'
behaviors, with teens emphasizing the restrictions of their freedoms and
parents emphasizing, instead, conventional and prudential concerns (for
reviews of this research, see Smetana, 1997, 2006).

The research with Middle Eastern men and women, and with American
teens and parents, suggests that people occupying different positions in the
"social order" make, at least at times, different judgments of social practices.
The fact that these data refer to the contrasting perspectives of men versus
women and of teens versus parents should not, however, be taken to mean
that individuals' distinct perspectives on social conflicts are necessarily dic-
tated by culturally established power differentials or by relatively stable
differences in family status, age, knowledge, or experience. In the normal
course of social interactions, most people are likely to find themselves occupying one position in some contexts and another position in others. This
is particularly salient with regards to interpersonal moral conflicts, as most
people occupy the victim's position in some cases and that of perpetrator
(or, at least, of perceived perpetrator) in others.

The fact that children occupy each of the two positions at different times
has been documented by a study (Smetana et al., 1999) in which maltreated
and nonmaltreated preschool children were observed during free play on
the school grounds until transgressions entailing physical harm, psychological harm, and unfairness occurred. Within a short time, the majority of
children (both maltreated and nonmaltreated) were observed acting in the
role of perpetrator (i.e., aggressing, inflicting psychological harm, or being
unfair) in some interactions and in the role of victim (i.e., as victims of

17

aggression, psychological harm, or unfairness) in others. Although children's construals and interpretations of their interpersonal conflicts were not directly assessed, the findings of this study provide indirect support to the notion that things do not look the same from both perspectives. In the short interviews following the observations, significant differences emerged in the evaluative judgments that victims and perpetrators made about the transgressions in which they had participated. Victims judged the transgressions to be more serious and more deserving of punishment than did perpetrators; perpetrators, in turn, judged the same transgressions to be more justifiable than did victims.

In other studies, preschoolers were found to reason differently about hypothetical transgressions in which they were described as the victim versus those in which they were described as the perpetrator (Dunn et al., 2000; Smetana, Kelly, & Twentyman, 1984; see also Eisenberg-Berg & Neal, 1981, for similar findings in regards to pro-social behavior). Children between the ages of 4 and 8 were also shown to use different linguistic devices, suggesting lesser and greater senses of agency, to describe situations in which they had angered or saddened someone and situations in which someone had angered or saddened them (Bamberg, 2001; see also Sedlak & Walton, 1982; Walton, 1985). Research by Arsenio and his colleagues (Arsenio & Lover, 1999; Arsenio et al., 2006), has also indicated that children recognize that victims and perpetrators have distinct emotional experiences (e.g., victims are sad or angry, perpetrators are happy or both happy and sad/regretful).

As a whole, findings from social and developmental psychology support our proposition that perspective makes a difference in moral thinking. Even as some research has been conducted examining children's reports of their own interpersonal conflicts (e.g., Shantz, 1993; Murphy & Eisenberg, 2002), there has been no systematic research into how children construe and interpret their own interpersonal conflicts in which they had been in the position of victims or perpetrators. As we set out to document the systematic differences in the ways children of different ages interpret situations in which they had mistreated or hurt someone, and situations in which they had been hurt or mistreated, we sought a research methodology that would maximize our ability to identify the varied ways in which children construe and organize their own experiences. We turn, next, to describing the approach we have chosen.

II. THE PRESENT STUDY: RESEARCH STRATEGY AND METHODS

WHY NARRATIVES?

The analysis of children's narrative accounts of their own conflict experiences seemed well suited for our purposes for two reasons. First, as it is generally agreed, narratives bring to the fore the interpretive dimension of knowledge (Bruner, 1986, 2002; Polkinghorne, 1988, 1996). By assessing children's narrative accounts of their own interpersonal conflicts, it was possible to obtain information not only about children's moral evaluations of their experiences as victims and perpetrators, but also about the specific ways in which they constructed and interpreted those experiences. Furthermore, we regard children's narrative construals of their own experiences of interpersonal conflict as broadening significantly the lens through which moral development is understood. Bruner (1990) has argued that transgressive acts, in particular, require narrative justification. We go further and argue—and this is the second reason for thinking that narratives are particularly well suited for our purposes—that narratives (indeed, positioned narratives, to borrow from Bamberg's [1997, 2001] terminology) about concrete conflictive interactions, more than judgments about hypothetical situations, can render visible the features of social interactions that are at the basis of moral development and moral thinking.

The strategy adopted for this study consisted of asking children to furnish two narrative accounts, one of a time when they were hurt by a peer and one of a time when they hurt a peer. Because the same child furnished accounts from each perspective, this strategy allowed us to interpret the differences between the two accounts as being associated, not with different types of children, but with children's different perspectives. To examine how perspective differences get played out within the context of different developmental abilities, we included a broad age range (5–16 years). Evidence that even preschool children are able to recall past experiences and to furnish reasonably coherent accounts of those events (e.g., Fivush, Gray, & Fromhoff, 1987; Fivush, Haden, & Adams, 1995; McCabe & Peterson, 1991) suggested that it would be feasible to use this strategy with young children. The within-subject design we used allowed us to disentangle what might be age-related differences in perspective-taking ability from those differences associated with the child's perspective in the conflict situation.

In spite of the burgeoning interest of psychologists in autobiographical narratives, little agreement exists regarding how narrative accounts can best be analyzed. Whereas content coding represents by far the dominant approach to narrative analysis (see McLean, Pasupathi, & Pals, 2005), narratives can also be examined in terms of their structure and coherence (e.g., McCabe & Peterson, 1991; Stein & Albro, 1997). Because there is evidence that narrative content and coherence provide non-redundant and complementary information about the ways in which events are represented and interpreted (Peterson & McCabe, 1983), we have included both types of analyses.

The analysis of narrative content, which has been reliably used with children's (e.g., Fivush et al., 1987; Toth, Cicchetti, Macfie, Rogosch, & Maughan, 2000) and adults' (e.g., Baumeister, Stilwell, & Wotman, 1990) narratives, provides detailed information about the "what" and "why" of interpersonal harm situations as understood from each perspective by drawing attention to the specific features ("narrative elements") present in children's construals of a situation and their relative salience. As we have discussed in the previous chapter, there is evidence that children account, in their moral evaluations, for features such as intentions and consequences (e.g., Helwig & Turiel, 2002; Nelson Le-Gall, 1985; Shultz et al., 1986; Smetana, 2006), emotions (Arsenio & Lover, 1999; Arsenio et al., 2006), and beliefs (Wainryb, 1991; Wainryb & Ford, 1998; Wainryb et al., 1998) when information about these features is explicitly provided, but less is known about whether children actually consider these features spontaneously. The analysis of the contents of children's narratives can provide such information. This type of analysis can also shed light on whether children include different features in their construals from each perspective, as well as on how children actually view each of these features from different perspectives (i.e., the types of intentions, emotions, or beliefs that they spontaneously attribute to themselves and others).

Whereas moral development research has typically ignored the coherence of children's discourse, it is generally agreed, among those studying narratives, that the coherence of a narrative reflects the integration (or lack thereof) of different aspects of an experience (McAdams, 1996; Polkinghorne, 1988). The coherence of children's victim and perpetrator narratives can therefore provide additional information about the ways in which those experiences were represented. Given that research (e.g., Fivush et al., 1987; McCabe & Peterson, 1991; Toth et al., 2000) has shown that even preschool children are able to recall details of specific past experiences and to furnish reasonably coherent narratives of these events, it seems feasible to examine

20

narrative coherence as an additional source of information of children's construals of their experiences from different perspectives.

GENERAL HYPOTHESES

There are no compelling theoretical or empirical grounds for predicting the precise differences between children's victim and perpetrator narratives. Attribution research (e.g., Nisbett, 2005; Pronin et al., 2002; Ross, 1990; Ross & Ward, 1996) suggests that when speaking as victims and perpetrators children are likely to focus on and attend to different aspects of situations. The specific foci of victims and perpetrators cannot be predicted on the basis of attribution research, as this research has dealt with self-other, rather than victim-perpetrator, differences. It is likely that when children find themselves in the position of being the target of mistreatment, their own anger and frustration (what happened to *me*, what was done to *me*) are more immediately present, hence more salient, than elements such as the perpetrator's goals or intentions. By contrast, when children are the ones who inflicted harm on someone else, it seems likely that they would be more aware of their own goals and intentions (what *I* wanted, what *I* meant to do, what was standing in *my* way). At the same time, given the systematic evidence from moral development research (e.g., Smetana, 2006; Turiel, 1998) pointing to children's attunement to and concern about others' welfare, it is also likely that perpetrators might also retain an awareness and concern with the victim's plight. Furthermore, even though being the target of harm or unfairness is likely to be very upsetting, the experience of having caused pain or distress to others is also likely to be distressing and confusing.

Accordingly, our expectations were that the construals of victims and perpetrators would differ on multiple levels. We expected victim narratives to include more references to elements of the narrator's own (i.e., the victim's) experience (desires, feelings, thoughts) than to elements of the perpetrator's experience. We also expected that victim narratives would be relatively coherent, as the victim's "story" is likely to be fairly linear (e.g., "she did something to me, and this is how I felt"). Perpetrator narratives, by contrast, were expected to include references to the narrator's own experience (e.g., their own desires, intentions, and feelings) as well as to references to the victim's experience (especially the victim's feelings). We thus expected perpetrator narratives to be comparatively less coherent, reflecting children's heightened distress as well as their need to integrate elements from their own and the victim's experiences. Differences between victims and perpetrators in their moral evaluations were also expected, with victims

21

making more unequivocally negative judgments than perpetrators (Smetana et al., 1999).

Age differences in children's construals of conflict situations were also expected. Based on research examining the development of children's narratives, we expected the narratives of younger children to be generally shorter and less detailed and elaborated (Fivush et al., 1987; McCabe & Peterson, 1991; Toth et al., 2000). Given research (e.g., Astington et al., 1988; Bartsch & Wellman, 1995; Wellman, 2002) indicating young children's limited understandings of the role of mental activity in experience, we expected their construals of conflict situations to include fewer references to psychological elements (e.g., intentions, mental states). Younger children's narratives were also expected to be, overall, less coherent (e.g., Fivush et al., 1987; McCabe & Peterson, 1991). Even as younger children's construals were expected to differ in their content and coherence from those of older children, we expected that the construals of victims and perpetrators would differ, in similar ways, at all ages. It was less clear what we should expect in terms of age differences in moral evaluations. Findings from moral development research (Smetana, 2006; Turiel, 1983, 1998) lead us to expect no age differences. However, if younger and older children construe conflict situations differently, it is possible that they might also judge those situations differently.

METHOD

Participants

The sample consisted of 112 participants, 14 males and 14 females in each of four grade levels: preschool (mean age = 4.8 years), first grade (mean age = 6.9 years), fifth grade (mean age = 10.9 years), and tenth grade (mean age = 16.2 years). Participants were of middle class and primarily Caucasian (71%; 18% Hispanic, 4% Asian, 3% African American, and 2% American Indian), and attended local daycare centers and public schools in a mid-size city in the western United States. Parental consent and participant assent were obtained for all participants.

Design and Procedure

Two narratives were elicited from each participant, one relating to a situation in which the participant was hurt by something a peer said or did ("Tell me about a time when a child you know well, like a friend, did or said something and you felt hurt by it. Pick a time you remember really well, and tell me everything you remember about that time"), and one relating to a situation in which the participant said or did something that hurt a peer. ("Tell me about a time when you did or said something, and a friend or a child you know well ended up feeling hurt by it. Pick a time that you remember really well, and tell me everything that you remember about that time.")

The decision to use a passive voice to elicit the narratives was deliberate, and concerned largely the narratives given from the perpetrator's perspective. Research on children's discourse about naturally occurring transgressions (e.g., Sedlak & Walton, 1982), as well as our own experience interviewing children, suggest that passive language (i.e., ". . . a time when you did . . . something, and a friend . . . ended up feeling hurt by it") may be more consistent with how children speak about their own wrongdoings than more active linguistic constructs (e.g., ". . . a time when you hurt someone" or "a time when you did something that hurt someone"). The probe used to elicit narratives from the victim's perspective was, naturally, designed to parallel the one used for perpetrator narratives. Narratives were elicited about incidents with friends or known peers (as opposed to unknown others), as these experiences are more likely to be represented and remembered in rich and detailed ways (Shantz, 1993).

The interviewer encouraged participants to continue speaking by using general prompts ("uh huh . . .," "and . . ."?) or by repeating verbatim part of what the child said ("So Susie grabbed your book . . ."). When the child appeared to have come to the end of his/her narrative, the interviewer asked "Is there anything else you remember about that time?" This procedure, used by researchers of children's narrative development (e.g., Peterson & McCabe, 1983), ensures that the interviewer provides no cues for either the content or the structure of the child's narrative. Following each account, participants were asked to evaluate the perpetrator's behavior as follows: "Do you think it was okay or not okay for [you/other child's name] to do [harmful behavior]? Why do you think it was [okay/not okay] for [you/him/her] to do that?"

The order for eliciting the victim and perpetrator narratives was counterbalanced within each age and gender group. Participants were individually interviewed in a private room at their school or home. Interviews were audio-taped, and were subsequently both digitized (to ease repeated listening) and transcribed. The transcripts were used for content analyses; for the purpose of coherence analyses, both transcripts and digitized interviews were used.

Scoring and Reliability

The total number of words per narrative was obtained using the LIWC, Linguistic Inquiry and Word Count (Pennebaker & Francis, 1999).

23

Narratives were analyzed for content and coherence. Two aspects of narrative content were scored, namely, the presence of specific narrative elements and the contents conveyed in each narrative element. Narrative coherence was scored in terms of six coherence markers and a global coherence score. As further indication of the structure of narratives, the number of shifts between elements pertaining to the experience of the victim to those pertaining to the experience of the perpetrator (and vice versa) was also calculated. Finally, moral judgments were scored. Details on each scoring system follow.

Presence of Narrative Elements

References to eight narrative elements were scored: harmful behavior (e.g., "this kid in my class called me stupid"), victim's response ("he went and told the teacher"), resolutions ("we made up and now we're friends again"), intentions (e.g., "I just wanted to get back at her for making fun of me"), narrator's mental states ("I thought maybe he was just joking around"), other child's mental states ("She really wanted to come on the camping trip"), narrator's emotions ("I was feeling really guilty about yelling at him"), and other child's emotions ("You could tell that it made him feel really sad"). A full description of each narrative element and examples from each perspective are included in Table 1. Within the narratives, each reference to a narrative element was recorded (for an example of the scoring of narrative elements within a narrative, see Appendix A). This procedure afforded the opportunity to obtain information not only about the presence of each narrative element in a narrative, but also about the salience of each narrative element (scored in terms of the proportional frequency with which each narrative element appeared in a narrative).

Content of Narrative Elements

The contents of each narrative element (e.g., harmful behavior, victim's response) were scored according to categories derived from previous scoring systems (e.g., Davidson et al., 1983) and further elaborated on the basis of the scoring of pilot data. References to harmful behaviors were scored with categories such as physical harm, offensive behavior, exclusion, and trust violation. References to the victim's response were scored using categories such as asked for help, retaliated, and withdrew. References to the event's resolution involved categories such as circumstantial resolutions, conflict resolved, and damage to relationship. References to the perpetrator's

24

TABLE 1

CATEGORIES USED FOR SCORING NARRATIVE ELEMENTS

Narrative Element	Description and Examples
Harmful behaviors	References to perpetrator's behavior or speech that resulted in harm to the victim (e.g., "One time Janie, my best friend, she said 'I'm not your friend anymore. I hate you,'" "Me and my friend were in a fight and I pushed him over")
Victim's responses	References to victim's actions following perpetrator's harmful behavior (e.g., "So I went inside and told the teacher that he hit me," "He got really mad after I said that, and he started yelling at me and calling me names")
Resolutions	References to event's denouement (e.g., "Then she ended up coming back and apologizing to me, so that was pretty much the end of the situation," "So we never really talked about it, and now we don't really ever talk anymore")
Narrator's mental states	Narrator's references to own thought processes (e.g., "I was thinking about it and I was like, 'How could I do that to my best friend?'" "I didn't want to say anything because I knew it would hurt her feelings")
Other child's mental states	References to the other child's thought processes. Thought processes were (a) communicated to narrator (e.g., "So she called me the next day and said 'That wasn't funny, I didn't realize you were joking, I thought you were serious'"), (b) inferred from behavior (e.g., "I could tell she just wanted to hang out with Kelly, because she was just ignoring me and stuff"), or (c) narrator did not indicate source (e.g., "He wanted to play a different game")
Narrator's emotions	Narrator's references to own feelings (e.g., "And that made me really mad," "I felt really sorry just because I betrayed her trust and I just felt bad about that")
Other child's emotions	References to other child's feelings. Emotions were (a) communicated to narrator (e.g., "So she told me that she felt really guilty for making fun of me"), (b) inferred from behavior (e.g., "I know he was hurt, like, he was crying"), or (c) narrator did not indicate source (e.g., "He seemed really angry")
Perpetrator's intentions	References to perpetrator's reasons for behaving as he/she did; does not require explicit use of words such as "intention," "purpose," or "reason" (e.g., "The reason behind that she broke up with me was the fact that she also wanted to go with my best friend," "I accidentally like broke one of his favorite rocks, like, I was running with it and I accidentally dropped it")

intentions were scored using categories such as intent to harm, retribution, incidental to pursuit of goal/preference, and impulsive. References to mental states were scored using categories such as desires/preferences, disbelief, and uncertainty. References to emotions were scored using categories such as sadness, anger, and guilt. (For a complete set of instructions for scoring the contents of narrative elements, including category descriptions and examples, see Appendix B). Scores were calculated in terms of the proportional use of each category.

Coherence Scoring

The categories used to score narrative coherence were developed based on the NAP (Narrative Assessment Profile; Bliss, McCabe, & Miranda, 1998). Although the NAP (as well as the SNAP, Strong's Narrative Assessment Procedure; Strong, 1998) has typically been used in clinical and educational settings to assess children exhibiting communicative impairments, similar coherence scales have also been used in research (e.g., Fiese et al., 1999). For our purposes, the NAP seemed preferable over Fiese's coherence scale because it is uniquely suited for scoring narratives produced by children of all ages. Based on the NAP (Bliss et al., 1998), six markers of coherence were identified and rated as inadequate or adequate: topic maintenance (i.e., are most utterances in the narrative on topic or tangential?), event sequencing (i.e., are events organized in chronological order or leap-frogging sequences?), completion (i.e., is enough information presented so that the narrative can be understood?), references to place and time (i.e., is the context of events adequately identified?), and false starts/fluency (i.e., do dysfluencies, such as false starts and retracing of words, interfere with the understanding of the narrative?). Each narrative was also assessed in its entirety, without reference to the coherence markers, as being generally coherent (i.e., sufficiently elaborated and fluent such that the main thrust of the event could be understood and was easy to follow) or incoherent (i.e., impoverished and dysfluent, such that it was hard to discern what the main events and who the main characters had been). All coherence scoring was conducted based on both the reading of transcribed narratives and repeated listening to the digitized audio recordings. (For a complete set of instructions for scoring narrative coherence, including examples of narratives scored as adequate and inadequate according to each coherence marker, as well as narratives scored globally as coherent and incoherent, see Appendix C.) Coherence scores were calculated in terms of the proportion of narratives scored as coherent along each marker and on the global score.

Shifts Between References to the Experience of the Victim and the Perpetrator

Victim and perpetrator narratives were also scored for the number of times that narrators shifted in their focus from narrative elements pertaining to the experience of the victim to those pertaining to the experience of the perpetrator (and vice versa). For this purpose, narrative elements were split into those that refer directly to the victim's experience (i.e., victim's emotions, victim's mental states, victim's response) and those that refer to the perpetrator's experience (i.e., perpetrator's emotions, perpetrator's mental states, perpetrator's intentions); references to the harmful behavior and to resolutions were omitted from this analysis because they cannot be unequivocally identified as referring to the victim's or the perpetrator's experience. Each shift from references pertaining to one party's experience to the other was counted and the total number of shifts was calculated.

Moral Judgments

The assessment of moral judgments included both evaluations and justifications. Evaluations were scored using a three-point Likert scale, with positive evaluations scored as "1," mixed as "2," and negative as "3." Justifications were scored based on categories used in previous moral development studies (e.g., Davidson et al., 1983), and further elaborated based on scoring of 15% of the interviews. Justifications (see Table 2) included such categories as harm (e.g., "It wasn't okay because it hurt my feelings"), justice (e.g., "It just isn't fair what he did"), and personal goals (e.g., "It was okay to say no because it wasn't comfortable for me to go with him to the dance"). The coding of mixed evaluations presented a specific challenge. In the past, mixed evaluations had been scored as comprising two justifications, one for each side of the evaluation (e.g., Killen et al., 2002; Smetana et al., 1991). So, for example, an act such as "eating lots of sweets" may be scored as "okay" because it is judged to be within the realm of personal choice but also as "not okay" because it is seen as imprudent. This type of coding allowed researchers to keep track of which aspects of the act were deemed "okay" and which "not okay," and of the types of concerns which tend to occur together. In the present study, we sought to identify the specific arguments that participants offered to justify a mixed evaluation. Based on pilot data, two such justification categories emerged. In reference to certain conflict situations which participants construed as entailing two competing claims, only one of which could prevail (e.g., "He wanted to play Nintendo but I wanted to make a puzzle," "She really wanted us to be boyfriend and girlfriend, but I still liked my ex-girlfriend"), participants' mixed reasoning (which we labeled "competing desires") referred to both

27

TABLE 2

Categories Used for Scoring Justifications

Categories	Descriptions and Examples
Harm	References to harmful consequences to victim (e.g., "It wasn't okay because it hurt my feelings," "It wasn't okay because it made her feel really bad")
Justice	Appeals to justice (e.g., "It's not fair because everyone should be treated the same," "It wasn't fair because you should invite everyone, even if they're not good at basketball")
Personal goals	References to the legitimacy of perpetrator's preferences and goals (e.g., "I guess it was okay because he doesn't have to play with kids he doesn't like," "It was okay not to pick her because I wanted to win the game")
Necessary harm	References to behavior that was both necessary and harmful (e.g., "It was right that I said that to her, she needed to be told, but the way I said it was really mean and it hurt her feelings")
Competing desires	References to competing legitimate claims or desires (e.g., "It was kind of okay that I said no, but kind of not okay, because she wanted to play Barbies and I wanted to play animals, but we couldn't do both")
No intent to harm	References to perpetrator's actions being accidental, intended to aid the victim, or intended to avoid negative outcomes (e.g., "It was okay, because I was trying to help her learn to stand up for herself," "It was okay because it was just an accident, she didn't mean to hit me")
Rules and authority	Appeals to expectations of authorities or the existence of rules (e.g., "It wasn't okay, because she could get in big trouble for that," "It's not okay, because there's a rule that says you have to let everybody play")
Unelaborated	Justifications which were not sufficiently detailed to be scored (e.g., "Because it's just not okay to do that")

the legitimacy of the desires (e.g., "There's nothing wrong with wanting to make a puzzle,") and the harm that fell upon the victim (e.g., "But it meant that my friend's feelings would get hurt"). In the other type of mixed reasoning (which we labeled "necessary harm"), participants suggested that the reasons for the perpetrator's actions were legitimate, but the actions themselves resulted in harm (e.g., "Well, it was not okay, because the way I yelled at her really hurt her feelings, but she also really needed to be told before she lost any more friends," "I don't think I should have said it as harshly because she was so hurt, but I think that giving her that message was a good thing to do"). Multiple justifications were allowed; scores were calculated in terms of the proportional use of each category.

Scoring Reliability

Scoring reliability was assessed through the independent scoring of 20% of the transcripts by a second judge. Inter-rater reliability for narrative elements and their contents was 87.2% for the scoring of Harmful Behaviors (Cohen's $\kappa = .806$), 85.5% for the scoring of Victim's Response (Cohen's $\kappa = .823$), 85.2% for the scoring of Resolutions (Cohen's $\kappa = .810$), 84.4% for the scoring of Intentions (Cohen's $\kappa = .808$), 96.7% for the scoring of Narrator's Mental State (Cohen's $\kappa = .956$), 100% for the scoring of Other Child's Mental State, 97.2% for the scoring of Narrator's Emotions (Cohen's $\kappa = .965$), and 100% for the scoring of Other Child's Emotions. Inter-rater reliability for coherence markers was 94.0% for the scoring of Topic Maintenance (Cohen's $\kappa = .840$), 96.0% for the scoring of Event Sequencing (Cohen's $\kappa = .852$), 92.0% for the scoring of Completion (Cohen's $\kappa = .826$), 98.0% for the scoring of References to Place (Cohen's $\kappa = .949$), 98.0% for the scoring of References to Time (Cohen's $\kappa = .959$), and 92.0% for the scoring of False Starts (Cohen's $\kappa = .817$). Inter-rater reliability for the global coherence score was 85.4% (Cohen's $\kappa = .767$). Inter-rater reliability was 96.7% for the scoring of act evaluations (Cohen's $\kappa = .952$) and 90.9% for the scoring of justifications (Cohen's $\kappa = .808$).

Analytic Strategy

Analyses were conducted on each measure of content and coherence and on the moral judgments, by perspective, age, and gender, with perspective as a repeated measure. Preliminary analyses including the order in which narratives were elicited (i.e., victim–perpetrator or perpetrator–victim) as an additional between-subject variable yielded only 3 out of 45 significant effects; order was excluded from all subsequent analyses. ANOVA-based procedures were adopted because they have been shown to be more appropriate for analyzing this type of data than are loglinear-based procedures, as the latter run into a distinct estimation problem (Wainryb, Shaw, Laupa, & Smith, 2001). Mean moral evaluations were analyzed using ANOVA. MANOVAs, and subsequent repeated measures ANOVAs, were performed on all proportional scores (narrative elements, semantic categories, coherence scores, and moral justifications); unelaborated responses were not included in the analyses. For all analyses, post hoc comparisons using Duncan multiple-range tests, with an overall α level of .05, were performed to test significant between-subjects effects. Checks for skewness and kurtosis were conducted and, where appropriate, arcsine and logarithmic transformations were used. Analyses with transformed and untransformed data yielded identical results; results are presented with the untransformed data.

The results of these analyses are presented in three chapters. Chapter III focuses on the differences between narratives told from the victim's perspective and narratives told from the perpetrator's perspective; comparisons in terms of narrative content and narrative coherence are included in this section. In Chapter IV we discuss findings bearing on age differences in children's narrative construals, and consider whether the differences between narratives told from the victim's and the perpetrator's perspective remain constant with age. At the end of Chapter IV we consider jointly the findings from Chapters III and IV as we examine actual examples of typical victim narratives and perpetrator narratives given by children of different ages. Analyses comparing the narratives of boys and girls indicated that, on average, girls' narratives were longer than boys' narratives (mean word counts were $M = 218.3$, $SD = 173.8$ and $M = 133.6$, $SD = 80.2$ respectively; $F(1, 110) = 10.96$, $p = .001$, $\eta^2 = .09$), and included more detail (mean number of references were $M = 13.4$, $SD = 8.7$ and $M = 8.2$, $SD = 4.3$, respectively; $F(1, 110) = 16.05$, $p < .001$, $\eta^2 = .13$). Nevertheless, because girls' and boys' construals of their victim and perpetrator experiences were found not to differ significantly on any other measure, analyses by gender are not considered. Finally, in Chapter V we contrast the types of moral judgments that children make about the transgressions depicted in their victim and perpetrator narratives.

III. THE NARRATIVE ACCOUNTS OF VICTIMS AND PERPETRATORS

Based on the widely held assumption (e.g., Bruner, 1986, 2002; Polkinghorne, 1988, 1996) that narrative accounts reflect children's own representations and interpretations of their experiences, as well as on the data to be described below, we will show in this chapter that moral conflicts are not experienced in the same ways by victims and perpetrators or, more precisely, that children's construals of conflict situations when they are the targets of aggressive or unfair acts are different from their construals of similar situations in which they are those perpetrating the aggression. To be able to appreciate these differences, however, it is important to begin with some nontrivial similarities found between children's accounts of their own experiences as victims and perpetrators.

To begin with, accounts given from both perspectives were generally not different in length or amount of elaboration and detail. Analyses performed on the mean word count as measured by LIWC ($M = 190$, $SD = 204$ and $M = 162$, $SD = 112$, respectively, for victim and perpetrator narratives) and on the mean number of references to narrative elements ($M = 11.2$, $SD = 10.9$ and $M = 10.6$, $SD = 6.4$, respectively) yielded no significant differences between narratives told from the victim's and the perpetrator's perspectives. Victim and perpetrator narratives also featured similar types of incidents, largely instances of offensive behavior (46–40%, in victim and perpetrator narratives, respectively) and, to a lesser extent, instances of social exclusion (16–17%) and physical harm (17–11%). Although participants were not asked to rate how severe those incidents were, a cursory examination of the data indicated that only a minority of the narratives from both perspectives depicted incidents in which the physical or psychological consequences seemed quite severe, such as when a preschooler pushed another child down with force and made him bleed, or when a fifth grader told another child whose father had recently committed suicide to stop talking about him because "he's dead, it doesn't matter anymore." For the most part, narratives given from both perspectives depicted incidents with less severe consequences, such as when a child comments that another child's favorite movie was "a baby movie" (fifth grade), or someone is not allowed to shoot a hoop (first grade), or is ditched by a friend (tenth grade). It should also be noted that the types of incidents that children depicted as examples of their own interpersonal experiences as both victims and perpetrators tap into the same universe of moral experience typically studied using hypothetical stimuli. It is against this backdrop of similarities between the incidents depicted by victims and perpetrators, and between them and those routinely studied in moral development research, that the significant differences between victims' and perpetrators' views, to which we turn next, should be understood.

WHAT DO VICTIMS AND PERPETRATORS TALK ABOUT?

In spite of their similarities, narratives told from the victim and the perpetrator perspectives focused on different behavioral and psychological aspects of the experience. As shown in Table 3, different types of narrative elements were present, $F(8, 101) = 20.35$, $p < .001$, $\eta^2 = .62$, and salient, $F(7, 102) = 18.46$, $p < .001$, $\eta^2 = .56$, in narratives told from the victim and

TABLE 3

NARRATIVE ELEMENTS PRESENT AND SALIENT IN NARRATIVES, BY PERSPECTIVE

Narrative elements	Proportion of narratives in which narrative element was present		Proportional frequency of each narrative element (salience)	
	Victim	Perpetrator	Victim	Perpetrator
Harmful behaviors	1.00	1.00	$.41_a$	$.29_b$
(SD)	(.00)	(.00)	(.23)	(.19)
Victim's responses	.54	.54	.11	.09
(SD)	(.50)	(.50)	(.14)	(.11)
Resolutions	$.36_a$	$.48_b$	$.06_a$	$.09_b$
(SD)	(.48)	(.50)	(.10)	(.11)
Narrator's mental states	.60	.56	.11	.10
(SD)	(.49)	(.50)	(.11)	(.12)
Other child's mental states	$.38_a$	$.57_b$	$.05_a$	$.09_b$
(SD)	(.49)	(.50)	(.09)	(.11)
Narrator's emotions	$.67_a$	$.35_b$	$.15_a$	$.05_b$
(SD)	(.47)	(.48)	(.15)	(.09)
Other child's emotions	$.16_a$	$.71_b$	$.03_a$	$.15_b$
(SD)	(.38)	(.45)	(.08)	(.14)
Perpetrator's intentions	$.50_a$	$.73_b$	$.08_a$	$.14_b$
(SD)	(.50)	(.44)	(.11)	(.11)

Note.—Mean proportions in the same row that do not share subscripts differ at $p < .05$ in follow-up ANOVAs with perspective as a repeated measure. Mean proportions for salience may not add up to 1.00 due to rounding.

the perpetrator perspectives. As might be expected, given that participants were asked to provide narratives about situations in which interpersonal harm took place, all narratives given from both perspectives included at least one reference to the perpetrator's harmful behavior. Nevertheless, references to harmful behavior constituted 41% of all references provided in narratives told from the victim's perspective, as compared with only 29% of references provided in narratives told from the perpetrator's perspective, $F(1, 108) = 25.05$, $p < .001$, $\eta^2 = .19$, giving the impression that the harm inflicted and suffered is more salient to children when they consider situations in which they were the ones being hurt. References to other behavioral elements, such as the victim's response and the conflict's resolution made up, together, another 17–18% of children's narratives from each perspective (perpetrator narratives featured references to conflict resolution slightly more often than did victim narratives, $F(1, 108) = 6.18$, $p = .014$, $\eta^2 = .05$).

The actual contents of the behavioral elements included in children's construals are listed in Table 4. Even though, as stated above, references to harmful behaviors were more salient in victim narratives, victims and perpetrators referred largely to similar types of behaviors. As shown in Table 4, both victims and perpetrators depicted instances of offensive behavior (e.g., "... then one of his friends told me how, that I was too guy-ish," "I said to her that I didn't like the way she dressed and that she smelled funny"). Although not as frequent, incidents of exclusion were also present in narratives from both perspectives (e.g., "I do remember a time when one of my friends ditched me ...," "I think I remember that time when some-one was, um, talking to me and they said, um, I said, um, 'Stephan, I just don't want to play with you'"), as were incidents involving physical harm (e.g., "Um, one time Max hit me," "I didn't want to play and so I pushed him down"). Although incidents involving trust violation (e.g., lying, breaking promises, spreading rumors) were more common in victim than perpetrator narratives, $F(1, 108) = 7.42$, $p = .008$, $\eta^2 = .06$, their overall frequency was very low. Similarly, although infrequent overall, incidents depicting harmless behaviors that were construed as hurtful by the victim (e.g., "Well, I said something nice but they, they didn't hear so they thought I said a bad word") were found only in the narratives of perpetrators, $F(1, 108) = 18.48$, $p < .001$, $\eta^2 = .15$. The overall similarities in the types of behavioral elements depicted by victims and perpetrators extended also to their references to the victim's response and the conflict's resolution. Both victims and perpetrators depicted victims as responding by confronting the perpetrator, asking for help, or withdrawing. When victims or perpetrators referred to the outcome of the conflict, they spoke largely about positive resolutions. In all, then, it appears that victims and perpetrators view the "landscape of action" (Bruner, 1986) of

TABLE 4

BEHAVIORAL ELEMENTS: TYPES OF HARMFUL BEHAVIORS, VICTIM'S RESPONSES, AND
RESOLUTIONS, BY PERSPECTIVE (PROPORTIONS)

	Perspective	
Behavioral elements	Victim	Perpetrator
Harmful behaviors		
Physical harm	.17	.11
(SD)	(.34)	(.29)
Offensive behavior	.46	.40
(SD)	(.45)	(.44)
Exclusion	.16	.17
(SD)	(.35)	(.35)
Trust violation	.18$_a$	.09$_b$
(SD)	(.34)	(.24)
Injustice	.02$_a$	.08$_b$
(SD)	(.12)	(.26)
Harmless behavior	.00$_a$	.12$_b$
(SD)	(.00)	(.30)
Unelaborated	.02	.03
(SD)	(.13)	(.16)
Victim's responses		
Confronted perpetrator	.19	.13
(SD)	(.36)	(.30)
Withdrew	.13	.19
(SD)	(.30)	(.38)
Asked for help	.13	.08
(SD)	(.31)	(.25)
Retaliated	.04$_a$	.11$_b$
(SD)	(.18)	(.30)
Attempted to reconcile	.02	.00
(SD)	(.11)	(.04)
No overt response	.04	.03
(SD)	(.18)	(.17)
No reference	.45	.46
(SD)	(.50)	(.50)
Resolutions		
Circumstantial resolution	.07	.03
(SD)	(.25)	(.15)
Attempted reparation	.07$_a$	.17$_b$
(SD)	(.23)	(.32)
Conflict resolved	.15	.18
(SD)	(.34)	(.34)
Damage to relationship	.06	.11
(SD)	(.22)	(.28)
No reference	.64$_a$	.52$_b$
(SD)	(.48)	(.50)

Note.—Mean proportions in the same row that do not share subscripts differ at $p < .05$ in follow-up
ANOVAs with perspective as a repeated measure. Mean proportions within a narrative element may not
add up to 1.00 due to rounding.

TABLE 5

PSYCHOLOGICAL ELEMENTS: TYPES OF MENTAL STATES AND EMOTIONS ATTRIBUTED TO
NARRATOR AND OTHER CHILD, BY PERSPECTIVE (PROPORTIONS)

Psychological elements	Narrator		Other child	
	Victim	Perpetrator	Victim	Perpetrator
Mental states				
Construal	$.05_a$	$.13_b$	.17	.15
(SD)	(.15)	(.29)	(.35)	(.32)
Prescriptive beliefs	.06	.09	.00	.01
(SD)	(.19)	(.24)	(.00)	(.07)
Disbelief	$.05_a$	$.02_b$	.01	.01
(SD)	(.15)	(.10)	(.01)	(.04)
Uncertainty	.06	.02	.02	.00
(SD)	(.22)	(.12)	(.13)	(.00)
Desires/preferences	.24	.19	$.18_a$	$.33_b$
(SD)	(.39)	(.36)	(.37)	(.45)
Realizations	.14	.11	.02	.04
(SD)	(.31)	(.26)	(.11)	(.16)
No reference	.40	.45	$.62_a$	$.45_b$
(SD)	(.49)	(.50)	(.49)	(.50)
Emotions				
Sadness	$.36_a$	$.06_b$	$.04_a$	$.46_b$
(SD)	(.45)	(.23)	(.19)	(.47)
Guilt	$.01_a$	$.10_b$	.03	.00
(SD)	(.05)	(.28)	(.16)	(.00)
Anger	.10	.15	$.09_a$	$.17_b$
(SD)	(.28)	(.34)	(.29)	(.35)
Unelaborated negative	$.20_a$	$.04_b$	$.01_a$	$.09_b$
(SD)	(.38)	(.19)	(.09)	(.25)
No reference	$.33_a$	$.65_b$	$.84_a$	$.29_b$
(SD)	(.47)	(.48)	(.37)	(.46)

Note.—Mean proportions in the same row that do not share subscripts differ at $p < .05$ in follow-up
ANOVAs with perspective as a repeated measure. Mean proportions within a narrative element may not
add up to 1.00 due to rounding.

their interpersonal conflicts in very similar ways, with the exception that
victims tend to refer more repeatedly to the harm fallen on them.

What about the "landscape of consciousness?" As can be seen in Table 3,
about half the references in the construals from each perspective (42%
and 53%, respectively, for victims and perpetrators) related, not to behavioral elements, but to psychological elements, such as intentions, thoughts,
and emotions—both the narrator's own and those of the other child.

In general, about half of the narratives (55–60%) from each perspective
included references to the narrator's own mental states. As shown in
Table 5, regardless of the perspective from which they spoke, children most
commonly described what they wanted and liked (e.g., "I still wanted to

fight," "I didn't like her very much") or talked about realizations that came about during the event (e.g., "... and just then I knew what I had to do," "... and then I figured out that he didn't have any friends"). In addition, when speaking from the perpetrator's perspective, children referred more often to their own understandings or construals of the situation (e.g., "I thought I'd never be able to find one just like that one"), $F(1, 108) = 7.16$, $p = .009$, $\eta^2 = .06$, and when speaking from the victim's perspective they described themselves as being in a state of disbelief (e.g., "So I broke up with him and then she went out with him, and I was like, 'Oh my God, how could you *do* that?'"), $F(1, 108) = 4.11$, $p = .045$, $\eta^2 = .04$.

Beyond the general similarities in how children depicted their own wants, thoughts, and beliefs, the landscape of consciousness they conjured as victims was significantly different from the one they conjured as perpetrators. When speaking as victims, children referred largely to their own emotions; when speaking as perpetrators, their intentions took center stage. As shown in Table 3, references to the narrator's own emotions were more frequent in narratives told from the victim's perspective, $F(1, 108) = 28.44$, $p < .001$, $\eta^2 = .21$, and made up 15% of all references in the victim narratives, but only 5% of references in the perpetrator narratives, $F(1, 108) = 41.12$, $p < .001$, $\eta^2 = .28$. Victims, more often than perpetrators, described themselves largely as feeling sad, $F(1, 108) = 35.44$, $p < .001$, $\eta^2 = .25$, or generally unwell, $F(1, 108) = 19.27$, $p < .001$, $\eta^2 = .15$, but rarely depicted themselves as having felt angry (see Table 5). Children's emotions as perpetrators, when present, referred largely to guilt (indeed, guilt appeared more often in the narratives of perpetrator than of victims, $F(1, 108) = 11.82$, $p = .001$, $\eta^2 = .10$, and anger (although anger was slightly more frequent in the narratives of perpetrators than in those of victims, this difference was not statistically significant).

Whereas perpetrators referred to their own emotions infrequently, their own intentions were central to their construals. Indeed, references to intentions were more frequent, $F(1, 108) = 17.32$, $p < .001$, $\eta^2 = .14$, and more salient, $F(1, 108) = 16.22$, $p < .001$, $\eta^2 = .13$, in perpetrator than in victim narratives (see Table 3). Perpetrators often explained their own actions in terms of accidents or retribution. For example, perpetrators explained that "we were going and I tripped and I accidentally pushed him, and then he got mad at me ... But I did it on accident," or that "I telled [sic] a joke on Cindy...cause she did something mean to me one day and so I played a bad joke on her." Not unexpectedly, both these types of reasons were invoked more frequently by perpetrators than by victims, $Fs(1, 108) = 21.00$ and 17.61, $ps < .001$, $\eta^2 = .16$ and $.14$, respectively (see Table 6).

Whereas notions bearing on retribution and accidental injury have been a long-standing part of moral development research, the reason that

TABLE 6

PSYCHOLOGICAL ELEMENTS: TYPES OF INTENTIONS ATTRIBUTED TO PERPETRATOR, BY
PERSPECTIVE (PROPORTIONS)

Perpetrator's intentions	Perspective	
	Victim	Perpetrator
Incidental to pursuit of goal/preference	$.15_a$	$.26_b$
(SD)	(.35)	(.42)
Retribution	$.01_a$	$.15_b$
(SD)	(.09)	(.34)
Mistaken assumption	$.09_a$	$.03_b$
(SD)	(.09)	(.03)
Impulsive	.06	.06
(SD)	(.23)	(.20)
Intent to harm	$.08_a$	$.02_b$
(SD)	(.26)	(.12)
Unintentional	$.04_a$	$.20_b$
(SD)	(.19)	(.37)
Incomprehensible	$.07_a$	$.01_b$
(SD)	(.25)	(.08)
No reference	$.50_a$	$.27_b$
(SD)	(.50)	(.44)

Note.—Mean proportions in the same row that do not share subscripts differ at $p < .05$ in follow-up ANOVAs with perspective as a repeated measure. Mean proportions may not add up to 1.00 due to rounding.

perpetrators invoked most frequently was one that has not been considered in previous research. Consider the following two examples, one by a younger child and one by an older one:

> I didn't play with her because I kind of wanted to play with another friend because, well, I knew she would be sad, but I wanted to make new friends so I could have lots of friends.

> My friend and I were going to have a sleepover and it was about three hours before it started but then my other friend called me and he asked me if he if I wanted to go have a sleepover . . . I thought it would be a lot more fun if I went with my second friend, but I didn't want to really hurt my other friend's feelings too much, so I told my other friend that my parents said I couldn't go and I ended up going with my other friend.

Perpetrators, as illustrated by these examples, often depicted themselves as being engaged in pursuing their own goals or interests, rather than intending to hurt someone else, and explained the harm ensuing from their actions as being an incidental (although not unforeseen) consequence of actions that they had taken in pursuit of those goals. It is also noteworthy that whereas perpetrators invoked this type of explanation more often than

37

did victims, $F(1, 108) = 5.58$, $p = .020$, $\eta^2 = .05$, this was also the most common explanation offered by those victims who made references to the perpetrator's intentions. Many victims, it seems, also believed that their peers had caused them harm in the process of pursuing their own goals (e.g., "She wanted to watch her favorite show 'Arthur' and so she told the babysitter to put it on and so I didn't get to watch my show"). We shall have more to say about this sort of "not-quite-intentional but not-quite-unintentional" type of harm later in this *Monograph*.

Describing the prevalence of intentions, however, does not convey a full picture of perpetrators' mental landscape. For, unlike the victims' self-referential focus, the landscape of consciousness of perpetrators was broader. Indeed, 71% of perpetrator narratives included at least one reference to the other child's emotions, as compared with only 16% of victim narratives, $F(1, 108) = 136.51$, $p < .001$, $\eta^2 = .56$ (see Table 3). As shown in Table 5, perpetrators, more often than victims, noted that the other child had felt sad, $F(1, 108) = 86.53$, $p < .001$, $\eta^2 = .45$, and to a lesser extent angry, $F(1, 108) = 4.90$, $p = .029$, $\eta^2 = .04$ (attributions of mixed emotions were infrequent). The construals of perpetrators (more often than those of victims, $F(1, 108) = 8.23$, $p = .005$, $\eta^2 = .07$) also included references to what the other child may have believed or may have been thinking (see Table 3). In fact, when children spoke as perpetrators they referred to the other child's mental states as often as they did to their own. References to the other child's desires and preferences (e.g., "he wanted to watch cartoons," "she would just rather hang out with her new friends"), especially, were more frequent in perpetrator than in victim narratives, $F(1, 108) = 8.23$, $p = .005$, $\eta^2 = .07$.

When taken together, the findings bearing on victims' and perpetrators' construals of the psychological elements of conflict situations suggest two things. First, narratives told from the perpetrator perspective involved a dual focus, including elements relating both to the perpetrator's own experience and to the experience of the other child. Second, in their construals of interpersonal conflict situations, children always maintained at least a partial focus on the suffering of the person who was harmed (the victim) regardless of from which perspective the narrative was told. In fact, overall, references to the victim's emotions were more frequent than references to the perpetrator's emotions, $F(1, 108) = 117.55$, $p < .001$, $\eta^2 = .52$, regardless of which role the narrator played. We shall return to both of these issues later.

Having described in great detail *what* victims and perpetrators talk about—that is, what elements of the conflict situation come into focus as children consider incidents in which they had been the targets of harm and incidents in which they had been the perpetrators—we turn next to see what can be learned from the structure and coherence of children's narratives. We turn, that is, to *how* victims and perpetrators talk about their experiences.

AND HOW DO THEY TALK ABOUT IT?

As it is generally agreed that a narrative's organization and coherence reflects the integration (or lack thereof) of different aspects of an experience (McAdams, 1996; Polkinghorne, 1988), we expected that by listening to *how* victims and perpetrators talk about their experiences, we might learn more about children's construals of those experiences. To this end, narratives provided from the victim's and the perpetrator's perspectives were compared along a number of indices of coherence.

One such measure was the number of shifts featured, in a narrative, from an element bearing on the experience of the victim (e.g., victim's emotions, victim's mental states, victim's response) to one bearing on the experience of the perpetrator (e.g., perpetrator's emotions, perpetrator's mental states, perpetrator's intentions), and vice-versa. Unlike other coherence indices we adopted, which were based on existing measures (e.g., Bliss et al., 1998; Fiese et al., 1999), the idea of merely counting the number of shifts from one perspective to the other emerged from listening to children in our sample account for incidents from each perspective (we mean "listening" in a literal sense, as we actually listened to the digitized interviews). Almost as soon as we started listening to the recording of narratives it became apparent that some narratives followed what seemed to be a linear structure, as it were, and others seemed to "leapfrog" (Bliss et al., 1998). This difference was not only immediately evident but also quite compelling in its effect on us as listeners.

At first we thought that these two distinctive organizations, let's call them "linear" and "leapfrogging," could be captured in terms of typical measures of coherence such as fluency, sequencing, or topic maintenance. Further examination revealed that, whereas many of these leapfrogging narratives could be coded as suffering from inadequate fluency, they could not be reliably distinguished in terms of event sequencing or topic maintenance. Some of the "leapfrogging" narratives were not adequate in these regards, but many were. It appeared then that we were onto something that was not adequately captured by common coherence indices. For the leapfrogging in these narratives, it seemed, was not random. It was, rather, a going back and forth between considering something related to, say, the narrator, and something related to the other party in the conflict, and back again. Thus emerged the idea of counting the number of shifts between the two perspectives. When compared in this respect, narratives told from the perpetrator's perspective featured, on the average, more shifts ($M = 1.98$, $SD = 2.00$) than narratives told from the victim's perspective ($M = 1.53$, $SD = 1.85$), $F(1, 108) = 4.31$, $p = .040$, $\eta^2 = .04$. Furthermore, whereas the majority of narratives told from the perpetrator's perspective (71%) in-

TABLE 7

PROPORTION OF NARRATIVES RATED AS COHERENT ON SIX COHERENCE MARKERS, BY
PERSPECTIVE

Coherence markers	Perspective	
	Victim	Perpetrator
Topic maintenance	.82	.78
(SD)	(.39)	(.42)
Event sequencing	.88	.85
(SD)	(.33)	(.36)
Completion	.54$_a$	.41$_b$
(SD)	(.50)	(.49)
References to place	.80	.75
(SD)	(.41)	(.44)
References to time	.62$_a$	.48$_b$
(SD)	(.49)	(.50)
False starts and fluency	.79$_a$	.58$_b$
(SD)	(.41)	(.50)

Note.—Mean proportions in the same row that do not share subscripts differ at $p < .05$ in follow-up
ANOVAs with perspective as a repeated measure.

cluded at least one shift in focus from their own experience to the experience of their victims, or vice-versa, with nearly 20% including between four and six shifts, 42% of narratives told from the victim perspective did not include even one such shift, and only 8% included four to six shifts.

Additional analyses were conducted comparing victim and perpetrator narratives along well-established markers of coherence. The MANOVA yielded a significant effect for perspective, $F(6, 103) = 5.35$, $p < .001$, $\eta^2 = .24$. As shown in Table 7, the majority of narratives were judged to be adequate in terms of topic maintenance, event sequencing, and references to place. This is to say that, on the average, most children's utterances and references in each narrative were relevant to the incident depicted, rather than digressive or tangential, and that narratives from both perspectives were organized in such a way that it was possible to understand the setting of the incident and follow the chronology of events. Victim and perpetrator narratives, however, differed in regards to completion, $F(1, 108) = 4.96$, $p = .028$, $\eta^2 = .04$, references to time, $F(1, 108) = 5.77$, $p = .018$, $\eta^2 = .05$, and false starts, $F(1, 108) = 18.21$, $p < .001$, $\eta^2 = .14$. Even as victim and perpetrator narratives did not differ in length or in the number of references they included, victim narratives, it was found, were more complete and elaborated, and more fluent, than perpetrator narratives.

Because narratives may be adequate along some coherence markers but inadequate along others, with certain patterns of incoherence being more disruptive than others, narratives were also rated in their entirety (globally) as incoherent or coherent; this rating was done independently from the rating of each coherence marker. On this global measure of coherence, too, more victim narratives than perpetrator narratives (58% vs. 35%) were judged to be coherent, $F(1, 108) = 17.22$, $p < .001$, $\eta^2 = .14$.

TWO PERSPECTIVES ON THE MORAL WORLD

As we proposed at the outset, moral conflicts are not experienced in the same ways by the perpetrators of harm and by their targets. Whereas being the target of aggression or unfairness brings into sharp focus the child's own experience, being the one who inflicts pain or distress on another person appears to spotlight aspects of both the perpetrator's and the victim's experiences—a dual focus that seems to be associated with a lack of coherence. We suggest, based on the evidence concerning the multiple differences between children's victim and perpetrator narratives, that the experiences of victims and perpetrators exhibit two distinct gestalts. Let us consider some of this evidence.

Narratives told from the victim's perspective were largely construed around the victim's own experience. Victims made repeated references to the harm inflicted on them (e.g., "This kid in my class was picking on me . . . he kept calling me names . . . I told him I didn't like it but he just kept on picking on me") and depicted themselves as having felt sad. (Unexpectedly, victims rarely depicted themselves as having felt angry. It may be that anger, being a more action-oriented emotion than sadness, is experienced during the conflict but dissipates with time; perpetrators, in fact, often depicted victims as angry. It may, alternatively, be that children selected victim experiences which left them feeling sad rather than angry, although why that may be is hard to discern). Their narrow focus on their own thwarted wants and feelings was also evidenced in what victims did *not* include in their narratives. Most notably, only 16% of children included, in their victim narratives, references to the perpetrator's emotions. In light of research indicating that children do make judgments about the perpetrator's emotions (with children younger than 6–8 thinking that perpetrators feel happy, and older children judging that perpetrators are likely to experience conflicting emotions [Arsenio & Lover, 1995; Arsenio et al., 2006]), the finding that victim narratives systematically overlooked the perpetrator's emotions can be seen as a bias associated with the victim's perspective; children occupying the victim's perspective are systematically blinded to something to which they would attend in other contexts. This conclusion can also be extended to victims' scarce references to intentions. Although moral development research (e.g., Harris & Nunez, 1996; Jones & Nelson-

41

Le Gall, 1995; Nunez & Harris, 1998; Schult, 2002; Shultz et al.,1986; Siegel & Peterson, 1998) has amply documented that children, even very young children, take intentions into account in their moral thinking and judge acts of intentional harm as more wrong than acts in which the harm was depicted as unintentional, only about half of the children referred to intentions when speaking from the victim's perspective. Although it is unlikely that children do not care whether others hurt them on purpose or not, this oversight on their part may be seen as yet another bias associated with the victim's construal of interpersonal conflicts.

In contrast to victims' largely self-referential focus, narratives told from the perpetrator's perspective featured a dual focus on both the victim's *and* the perpetrator's experiences. The victim's perspective appears to blind children to the other child's emotions; the perpetrator's role does not. On the contrary, the large majority of children, when speaking from the perpetrator's perspective, referred to the victim's sadness and anger. Given that emotions contribute to how children remember moral conflicts (Arsenio & Lover, 1995; Dunn & Slomkowski, 1992), and in light of research indicating that aggressive and conduct-disordered children construe conflict situations in ways that minimize the experience of the victim (Astor, 1994; Nucci & Herman, 1982; Slaby & Guerra, 1988; Tisak et al., 2006), the reliable attention to the victim's experience exhibited by perpetrators in our study merits notice.

Perpetrators' simultaneous consideration of both their own and the victims' experiences, also evidenced in the multiple shifts back and forth between foci, suggests that experiences as perpetrators are more complex for children, and perhaps more confusing and disorganizing, than are their experiences as victims. We do not, by saying this, mean that being a victim is "easy" or simple. What our data suggest is that, as perpetrators, children attend more to the complexity of the situation. Further indication of this was the relative incoherence of narratives told from the perpetrator's perspective (only 35% were rated as coherent), which reflects children's difficulty in integrating different aspects of the experience.

Taken together, these multiple findings suggest that children's construals of interpersonal conflicts indeed vary systematically, and in substantial ways, with the perspective from which they experienced those conflicts. Why might the same children inhabit such different worlds when they are victims and perpetrators? And what might these differences mean as far as their moral judgments? Before we can consider such questions, we must turn to examine how children of different ages construe their victim and perpetrator experiences and, importantly, whether the differences between victim and perpetrator narratives remain constant across a broad age range, as age-related differences and their developmental implications shall have a direct bearing on how we answer them.

42

IV. NARRATIVE ACCOUNTS AND DEVELOPMENT

As we have already discussed, research in moral development has, over the past few decades, demonstrated that starting at a young age, perhaps as young as 3, children reason that it is morally wrong to hurt or mistreat others, not because they may otherwise be punished, but rather because of their concerns with fairness and the well-being of persons (for reviews of the results of over 100 studies, see Helwig & Turiel, 2002; Smetana, 2006; Tisak, 1995; Turiel, 1998). By the age of 3, children already possess basic moral concepts (ways of thinking about welfare and justice) that are not contingent on nonmoral considerations, but prescriptive and generalizable, and insofar as children understand a situation as implicating an agent who intentionally mistreats or inflicts harm on an unwilling victim, they will bring their moral concepts to bear on it. Naturally, this suggests that *how* children come to understand that an event involves intentional harm should be of critical importance. Coupled with yet another mountain of evidence suggesting that young children, in their preschool and early elementary school years, have limited understandings of persons, their mental lives, and the relation between people's mental lives and their actions (e.g., Astington et al., 1988; Lalonde & Chandler, 2002; Wellman, 2002), the issue of how children of different ages in effect construe their own experiences of interpersonal conflict seems to gain crucial significance.

Against this backdrop, we consider two questions. First we ask about the differences, as well as any similarities, in the ways in which children of different ages construe their own experiences of interpersonal conflict in general. Next, we ponder how children of different ages construe their experiences as victims and perpetrators in particular.

WHAT DO YOUNGER AND OLDER CHILDREN SEE, AND WHAT DO THEY MISS, IN CONSTRUING THEIR INTERPERSONAL CONFLICTS?

Consistent with research concerning the still developing narrative abilities of young children (Fivush et al., 1987; McCabe & Peterson, 1991; Toth et al., 2000), we found that the narratives of preschoolers and, to a lesser extent, those of first graders, were shorter and less elaborated than those of their older peers. Analyses performed on the mean word count, as measured by LIWC, and on the mean number of references yielded significant age differences, $F(3, 108) = 19.60$, $p < .001$, $\eta^2 = .35$ and $F(3, 108) = 15.65$, $p < .001$, $\eta^2 = .30$ for mean number words and references, respectively. The narratives of preschoolers included fewer words ($M = 67.8$, $SD = 38.5$) and fewer references to narrative elements ($M = 5.0$, $SD = 2.1$) than those of first and fifth graders (M words = 150.5 and 185.3, $SD = 87.9$ and 77.2, and M references = 10.0 and 12.1, $SD = 4.8$ and 4.9) which, in turn, included fewer words and references than those of tenth graders (M words = 300.3, $SD = 194.8$ and M references = 16.2, $SD = 10.2$). An age difference was also found in the number of shifts made between references to the victim's and the perpetrator's experience, $F(3, 108) = 12.79$, $p < .001$, $\eta^2 = .26$, with younger children making fewer shifts than older ones (in order, M's = .73, 1.39, 2.04, and 2.86, SD's = .91, 1.39, 1.30, 1.67).

Likely of more consequence for our purposes was the finding that the narratives of younger and older children featured different elements, $F(24, 309) = 4.83$, $p < .001$, $\eta^2 = .27$. All narratives by preschoolers included at least one reference to the harmful behavior involved in the incident, but no other element was systematically present (see Table 8). In fact, references to harmful behavior made up half of the preschoolers' narratives, as compared with only about 28–33% of older children's narratives, $F(3, 108) = 9.36$, $p < .001$, $\eta^2 = .21$.

In keeping with findings from moral development research (Davidson et al., 1983; Shantz, 1987; Smetana, 2006; Turiel, 1998), the types of harmful behavior that children described (see Table 9) also varied with age, $F(18, 315) = 2.95$, $p < .001$, $\eta^2 = .14$, with instances of physical harm being more common in the narratives of preschoolers than in those of first graders, and very infrequent in the narratives of fifth and tenth graders, $F(3, 108) = 6.06$, $p = .001$, $\eta^2 = .14$, and incidents of trust violation being more frequent in the narratives of tenth graders than in those of fifth and first graders, and nonexistent in the narratives of preschoolers, $F(3, 108) = 9.26$, $p < .001$, $\eta^2 = .21$.

As compared with the narrow focus of preschoolers' narratives, the majority of narratives by tenth graders (75%) included references to either seven or eight narrative elements (see Table 8). Over two-thirds of tenth grade narratives included references to harmful behaviors as well as to the narrator's mental states and the perpetrator's intentions, and over half also included references to the narrator's emotions, the victim's response, and the other child's emotions and mental states. The narratives of first to tenth graders included more references than those of preschoolers to behavioral elements such as the victim's response and the resolution of the conflict,

44

TABLE 8

PROPORTION OF NARRATIVES THAT INCLUDED EACH NARRATIVE ELEMENT, BY AGE

Narrative elements	Age			
	Preschool	1st grade	5th grade	10th grade
Harmful behaviors	1.00	1.00	1.00	1.00
(SD)	(.00)	(.00)	(.00)	(.00)
Victim's responses	$.20_a$	$.70_b$	$.70_b$	$.59_b$
(SD)	(.25)	(.37)	(.31)	(.33)
Resolutions	$.21_a$	$.52_b$	$.50_b$	$.45_b$
(SD)	(.31)	(.36)	(.38)	(.38)
Narrator's mental states	$.21_a$	$.50_b$	$.73_c$	$.88_c$
(SD)	(.25)	(.36)	(.32)	(.26)
Other child's mental states	.34	.54	.50	.54
(SD)	(.27)	(.38)	(.33)	(.38)
Narrator's emotions	$.36_a$	$.45_{ab}$	$.61_{bc}$	$.63_c$
(SD)	(.31)	(.34)	(.39)	(.31)
Other child's emotions	$.29_a$	$.30_a$	$.57_b$	$.57_b$
(SD)	(.31)	(.31)	(.27)	(.27)
Perpetrator's intentions	$.39_a$	$.54_{ab}$	$.70_{bc}$	$.84_c$
(SD)	(.31)	(.42)	(.34)	(.23)

Note.—Mean proportions in the same row that do not share subscripts differ at $p < .05$ in Duncan multiple-range tests.

Fs$(3, 108) = 14.29$ and 5.12, $p < .001$ and $p = .002$, η^2s $= .28$ and $.13$, respectively (see Table 9). Of potentially greater significance were the findings indicating that the large majority of fifth and tenth graders, as compared with only a small minority of preschoolers, included in their narratives references to intentions, mental states, and emotions. References to intentions, for example, were present in the majority of narratives by fifth graders (70%) and tenth graders (84%), but in only 54% of narratives by first graders and 39% of narratives by preschoolers, $F(3, 108) = 9.96$, $p < .001$, $\eta^2 = .22$. Similarly, fifth and tenth graders included in their narratives references to their own (i.e., the narrator's) mental states, $F(3, 108) = 25.83$, $p < .001$, $\eta^2 = .42$, and to their own emotions, $F(3, 108) = 6.21$, $p = .001$, $\eta^2 = .15$, as well as to the other child's emotions, $F(3, 108) = 8.29$, $p < .001$, $\eta^2 = .19$, more often than did younger children.

The finding that preschoolers so rarely refer to mental states in their descriptions of conflict situations is entirely consistent with a considerable body of evidence bearing on young children's constrained understandings of the working of minds (e.g., Astington, 2001; Lalonde & Chandler, 2002; Wellman, 2002). It stands to reason that young children, who do not comprehend the representational nature of the mind and fail to see the distinction between actions or outcomes and mental states, would not see the

TABLE 9

BEHAVIORAL ELEMENTS: TYPES OF HARMFUL BEHAVIORS, VICTIM'S RESPONSES, AND
RESOLUTIONS, BY AGE (PROPORTIONS)

Behavioral elements	Age			
	Preschool	1st grade	5th grade	10th grade
Harmful behaviors				
Physical harm	$.29_a$	$.16_b$	$.06_c$	$.06_c$
(SD)	(.32)	(.27)	(.14)	(.14)
Offensive behavior	.35	.38	.49	.50
(SD)	(.28)	(.34)	(.34)	(.34)
Exclusion	.22	.20	.14	.09
(SD)	(.28)	(.28)	(.26)	(.19)
Trust violation	$.00_a$	$.09_b$	$.15_b$	$.29_c$
(SD)	(.00)	(.21)	(.25)	(.27)
Injustice	.08	.07	.04	.00
(SD)	(.18)	(.18)	(.12)	(.00)
Harmless behavior	.02	.08	.10	.04
(SD)	(.09)	(.17)	(.18)	(.14)
Unelaborated	.04	.02	.02	.02
(SD)	(.19)	(.09)	(.09)	(.09)
Victim's responses				
Confronted perpetrator	.08	.16	.17	.22
(SD)	(.18)	(.21)	(.24)	(.30)
Withdrew	$.05_a$	$.24_b$	$.22_b$	$.13_{ab}$
(SD)	(.16)	(.32)	(.31)	(.20)
Asked for help	.06	.17	.12	.07
(SD)	(.16)	(.26)	(.21)	(.16)
Retaliated	.02	.12	.12	.05
(SD)	(.09)	(.21)	(.25)	(.13)
Attempted to reconcile	.00	.01	.03	.01
(SD)	(.00)	(.06)	(.10)	(.03)
No overt response	$.00_a$	$.01_a$	$.04_a$	$.11_b$
(SD)	(.00)	(.04)	(.13)	(.18)
No reference	$.79_a$	$.30_b$	$.30_b$	$.41_b$
(SD)	(.25)	(.37)	(.31)	(.33)
Resolutions				
Circumstantial	$.00_a$	$.13_b$	$.05_{ab}$	$.02_a$
(SD)	(.00)	(.26)	(.12)	(.09)
Attempted reparation	.03	.17	.16	.11
(SD)	(.10)	(.22)	(.19)	(.20)
Conflict resolved	.15	.17	.12	.22
(SD)	(.33)	(.23)	(.17)	(.31)
Damage to relationship	$.04_a$	$.05_a$	$.16_b$	$.10_{ab}$
(SD)	(.13)	(.17)	(.23)	(.17)
No reference	$.79_a$	$.48_b$	$.50_b$	$.55_b$
(SD)	(.35)	(.32)	(.38)	(.42)

Note.—Mean proportions in the same row that do not share subscripts differ at $p < .05$ in Duncan multiple-range tests. Mean proportions within a narrative element may not add up to 1.00 because of rounding.

need to provide information about their own or their partners' mental states; such information might be seen as superfluous if mental states are "copies" of actions or outcomes in the world (Wainryb & Brehl, in press).

Even once children do begin to describe the "landscape of consciousness" (Bruner, 1986), we found, consistent with findings suggesting that children's understandings of the mind continue to develop well beyond their preschool years (Lalonde & Chandler, 2002), that there were differences not only in the relative frequency with which younger children and their older peers included references to mental states in their narratives, but also in the types of mental states to which they referred. Indeed, whereas the narratives of first through tenth graders did not differ in terms of the types of behavioral elements included, such as the types of responses attributed to victims or the types of conflict resolution (see Table 9), differences were found in regards to the psychological elements (see Table 10). Age differences were found in both the types of mental states, $F(18, 315) = 5.04$, $p < .001$, $\eta^2 = .22$, and the types of emotions, $F(12, 321) = 2.54$, $p = .003$, $\eta^2 = .09$, considered. (The exception to this was intentions; even though older children made more references to intentions, children from first to tenth grade referred to the same types of intentions.)

So, for example, in keeping with the documented prevalence of desires and wants in the network of mental state concepts of the young child (e.g., Astington, 2001; Wellman, 2002), preschoolers referred almost exclusively to their own wants and likes (e.g., "I really wanted to play animals"). Older children, in comparison, were more likely to make references to more active forms of mentally engaging with the experience, depicting themselves as "figuring out" what was going on (e.g., "I thought about it and thought maybe he's just gonna take off without me"), $F(3, 108) = 5.70$, $p = .001$, $\eta^2 = .14$. As they become more aware that conflicts hinge not solely on how things really are, but on how they are construed, children in the fifth and tenth grades also referred (more often than younger children, $F(3, 108) = 6.30$, $p = .001$, $\eta^2 = .15$) to their own understandings or construals of the situation (e.g., "I had thought we were just joking around"), and tenth graders made more references than their younger peers to what they thought should have happened (e.g., "I think that if she's going to say that, she should come to me and ask me first") and to being in a state of disbelief because of what had happened (e.g., "We'd been friends for so long, I just couldn't believe she'd do that to me"), $F(3, 108) = 9.36$, $p < .001$, $\eta^2 = .21$, and $F(3, 108) = 10.12$, $p < .001$, $\eta^2 = .22$, respectively.

The differences between younger and older children's narratives extended beyond their contents. Given that research on children's narrative development has shown that the narratives of preschool children are generally rudimentary and become more complex, more coherent, and more

TABLE 10

PSYCHOLOGICAL ELEMENTS: TYPES OF MENTAL STATES AND EMOTIONS ATTRIBUTED TO
NARRATOR AND OTHER CHILD, BY AGE (PROPORTIONS)

Measure	Narrator				Other child			
	Preschool	1st grade	5th grade	10th grade	Preschool	1st grade	5th grade	10th grade
Mental states								
Construal	$.00_a$	$.04_a$	$.16_b$	$.16_b$	.07	.16	.18	.23
(SD)	(.00)	(.08)	(.25)	(.18)	(.16)	(.29)	(.26)	(.26)
Prescriptive beliefs	$.02_a$	$.01_a$	$.09_a$	$.17_b$	.00	.00	.00	.02
(SD)	(.09)	(.06)	(.19)	(.18)	(.00)	(.00)	(.00)	(.07)
Disbelief	$.00_a$	$.00_a$	$.04_a$	$.11_b$	.00	.00	.00	.04
(SD)	(.00)	(.02)	(.11)	(.13)	(.00)	(.00)	(.00)	(.13)
Uncertainty	.00	.02	.08	.06	.00	.00	.02	.02
(SD)	(.00)	(.09)	(.18)	(.14)	(.00)	(.00)	(.09)	(.09)
Desires/preferences	.20	.30	.20	.16	.26	.34	.26	.17
(SD)	(.25)	(.34)	(.26)	(.20)	(.27)	(.36)	(.28)	(.24)
Realizations	$.00_a$	$.12_b$	$.17_b$	$.20_b$	.00	.02	.04	.05
(SD)	(.00)	(.21)	(.24)	(.20)	(.00)	(.10)	(.11)	(.12)
No reference	$.79_a$	$.50_b$	$.27_c$	$.14_c$	.66	.48	.50	.48
(SD)	(.25)	(.36)	(.32)	(.27)	(.27)	(.40)	(.33)	(.37)
Emotions								
Sadness	.19	.18	.25	.22	.21	.23	.25	.31
(SD)	(.28)	(.22)	(.26)	(.23)	(.28)	(.28)	(.23)	(.25)
Guilt	$.00_a$	$.02_{ab}$	$.10_c$	$.08_{bc}$	.02	.00	.02	.02
(SD)	(.00)	(.09)	(.20)	(.17)	(.09)	(.00)	(.09)	(.09)
Anger	.09	.08	.14	.20	$.06_a$	$.05_a$	$.24_b$	$.17_{ab}$
(SD)	(.18)	(.18)	(.21)	(.27)	(.16)	(.16)	(.30)	(.28)
Unelaborated negative	.08	.17	.11	.12	.02	.02	.07	.08
(SD)	(.18)	(.24)	(.24)	(.21)	(.09)	(.09)	(.14)	(.18)
No reference	$.64_a$	$.55_a$	$.39_b$	$.38_b$	$.71_a$	$.70_a$	$.43_b$	$.43_b$
(SD)	(.30)	(.34)	(.39)	(.29)	(.32)	(.31)	(.26)	(.30)

Note.—Mean proportions in the same row that do not share subscripts differ at $p < .05$ in Duncan multiple-range tests. Mean proportions within a narrative element may not add up to 1.00 because of rounding.

richly detailed and elaborated over the course of development (Fivush et al., 1987; McCabe & Peterson, 1991; Toth et al., 2000), it was unsurprising to find that younger and older children's narratives also differed in terms of coherence. As shown in Table 11, the majority of narratives at each age group were judged to be adequate in terms of topic maintenance and event sequencing. Hence even the rudimentary accounts of preschoolers referred to a recognizable incident and provided a basic sense of what the incident was about. Nevertheless, age differences were found in regards to completion, $F(3, 108) = 6.16$, $p = .001$, $\eta^2 = .15$, references to place,

TABLE 11

PROPORTION OF NARRATIVES RATED AS COHERENT ON SIX COHERENCE MARKERS, BY AGE

Coherence marker	Age			
	Preschool	1st grade	5th grade	10th grade
Topic maintenance	.75	.73	.84	.87
(SD)	(.32)	(.32)	(.24)	(.26)
Event sequencing	.80	.86	.86	.93
(SD)	(.31)	(.27)	(.18)	(.27)
Completion	$.23_a$	$.46_b$	$.57_b$	$.63_b$
(SD)	(.32)	(.36)	(.38)	(.42)
References to place	$.50_a$	$.73_b$	$.88_{bc}$	$.98_c$
(SD)	(.38)	(.35)	(.29)	(.09)
References to time	$.30_a$	$.41_a$	$.68_b$	$.80_b$
(SD)	(.34)	(.39)	(.31)	(.34)
False starts and fluency	$.50_a$	$.75_b$	$.70_b$	$.80_b$
(SD)	(.41)	(.32)	(.39)	(.28)

Note.—Mean proportions in the same row that do not share subscripts differ at $p < .05$ in Duncan multiple-range tests. Mean proportions within a narrative element may not add up to 1.00 because of rounding.

$F(3, 108) = 13.41$, $p < .001$, $\eta^2 = .27$, references to time, $F(3, 108) = 12.51$, $p < .001$, $\eta^2 = .26$, and false starts, $F(3, 108) = 3.90$, $p = .011$, $\eta^2 = .10$. In each case, the narratives of younger children (especially those of preschoolers) were judged to be less detailed, less elaborated, and less fluent than the narratives of older children. An age difference was also found in the global measure of coherence; over half the narratives of older children (52–66%) but only a minority of narratives of younger children (30–38%) were rated as coherent, $F(3, 108) = 5.32$, $p = .002$, $\eta^2 = .13$.

In light of the assumption (Bruner, 1986, 2002; Polkinghorne, 1988, 1996) that narrative accounts reflect children's representations and construals of their experiences, we interpret these data to mean, quite compellingly, that the experience of moral conflict is different for younger and older children. We further suggest that this pattern of age-related findings cannot be adequately explained in terms of age differences in children's ability to take the perspective of others. Indeed, one of the central findings bearing on age differences was that young children did not merely overlook the *other* child's feelings and thoughts, but also *their own*. The scarcity of references to even their own psychological experience suggests that young children's difficulties lie not in accounting for someone else's perspective, but rather in accounting for mentalistic or psychological aspects of interpersonal conflicts, such as feelings, thoughts, and intentions (Astington, 2001; Bartsch & Wellman, 1995; Chandler & Lalonde, 1996; Lagatutta & Wellman, 2001; Wellman, 2002). Whereas young children thought of conflicts in terms of concrete behaviors, older children talked about their own and other children's mental states suggesting, implicitly, that they recognize that feelings and thoughts are relevant components of interpersonal conflicts.

We do not, of course, discount age differences in narrative coherence (Fivush et al., 1987; McCabe & Peterson, 1991; Toth et al., 2000), as they may well bear on the explanation of our findings. On the contrary, we rely strongly on the widely held assumption, among those working with narratives as a tool in psychological research (e.g., McAdams, 1996; Polkinghorne, 1988), that the coherence of a narrative reflects the extent to which the experiences depicted in the narrative are (or are not) integrated. On this basis, we suggest that young children were not merely telling less coherent stories. Rather, it is likely that their actual *experiences* were less coherent. We speculate further that young children's phenomenological experiences of moral conflict are less coherent because they are made up, as it were, of fragmented behavioral moments. Another way to put this is that younger children's failure to integrate various aspects of their conflict experiences is rooted in their poor understanding of the psychological aspects of interactions. We further speculate that it is those understandings that glue together behavioral moments into a coherent experience.

Given this pattern of findings on the widely divergent construals that younger and older children make of situations of moral conflict, one might be tempted to conclude that younger and older children should also make widely divergent moral judgments—something that would be inconsistent with the last 25 years of moral development research (e.g., Smetana, 2006; Turiel, 1998). This question will be addressed in the next chapter. First, we examine whether the narrative construals of younger and older children retain the distinction between victims and perpetrators.

THE STABILITY OF DIFFERENCES BETWEEN VICTIMS' AND PERPETRATORS' CONSTRUALS

Consider the findings thus far. The narratives made from the victim's and the perpetrator's perspectives differed on several dimensions of content and coherence, with perpetrator narratives featuring a more complex focus on the perspectives of the two parties involved in the conflict situation. The narratives of younger and older children also differed in terms of content and coherence, with the narratives of older children featuring a more complex focus that went beyond behavioral elements and included a consideration of both parties' mental states. Could this mean that older children's narratives, in their complexity and awareness of the emotions and construals of both parties, might all resemble perpetrator narratives? In other words, might the distinct features of victims' and perpetrators' narratives recede in the face of children's increased understandings of the mind? The short answer to this question is no. For children of all ages, victim narratives differed from perpetrator narratives on most measures.

Analyses conducted on the distribution of elements included in the narratives yielded no significant interactions of perspective and age. That is to say that narratives told from the victim's and the perpetrator's perspective differed in similar ways at each age group. As shown in Table 12, references to the perpetrator's harmful behavior were present in all narratives told from both perspectives. At all ages, references to intentions were more common in narratives given from the perpetrator's than from the victim's perspective, $Fs(1, 27) > 4.50$, $ps < .043$, $\eta^2 s > .14$. At all ages, too, references to the victim's emotions were more frequent than references to the perpetrator's emotions, $Fs(1, 27) > 17.76$, $ps < .001$, $\eta^2 s > .40$. Indeed, children in each age group referred to their own emotions more often when they were victims than when they were perpetrators, $Fs(1, 27) > 3.98$, $ps < .05$, $\eta^2 s > .13$, and referred more often to the other child's emotions when the

TABLE 12

PROPORTION OF NARRATIVES IN WHICH NARRATIVE ELEMENTS WERE PRESENT BY
AGE AND PERSPECTIVE

	Age and perspective							
	Preschool		1st grade		5th grade		10th grade	
Narrative elements	V	P	V	P	V	P	V	P
Harmful behaviors	1.00	1.00	1.00	1.00	1.00	1.00	1.00	1.00
(SD)	(.00)	(.00)	(.00)	(.00)	(.00)	(.00)	(.00)	(.00)
Victim's responses	.21	.18	.64	.75	.64	.75	.68	.50
(SD)	(.44)	(.39)	(.49)	(.44)	(.49)	(.44)	(.48)	(.51)
Resolutions	.25	.18	.50	.54	.29	.71	.39	.50
(SD)	(.42)	(.39)	(.51)	(.50)	(.46)	(.46)	(.49)	(.50)
Other child's mental states	.21	.46	.39	.68	.39	.61	.54	.54
(SD)	(.42)	(.51)	(.50)	(.48)	(.50)	(.50)	(.51)	(.51)
Narrator's mental states	.18	.25	.57	.43	.71	.75	.93	.82
(SD)	(.39)	(.44)	(.50)	(.50)	(.46)	(.44)	(.26)	(.39)
Narrator's emotions	.50	.21	.64	.25	.71	.50	.82	.43
(SD)	(.51)	(.39)	(.49)	(.44)	(.46)	(.51)	(.36)	(.51)
Other child's emotions	.11	.46	.07	.54	.21	.93	.25	.89
(SD)	(.32)	(.51)	(.26)	(.51)	(.44)	(.26)	(.44)	(.26)
Perpetrator's intentions	.25	.54	.43	.64	.57	.82	.75	.93
(SD)	(.44)	(.51)	(.50)	(.48)	(.50)	(.39)	(.42)	(.26)

Note.—V, victim perspective; P, perpetrator perspective.

other child was the victim rather than the perpetrator, F's$(1, 27) > 15.68$, p's$ < .001$, η^2's$ > .37$.

The one exception to this pattern emerged in terms of the relative coherence of victim and perpetrator narratives among younger and older children. As indicated by a significant age × perspective interaction, $F(3, 108) = 3.50$, $p = .02$, $\eta^2 = .09$, victim narratives were more coherent than perpetrator narratives among first, fifth, and tenth graders but not among preschoolers, whose narratives tended to be equally incoherent from both perspectives (the interaction was significant for the overall coherence score, but not for each coherence marker separately). Indeed, the large majority (61–71%) of the victim narratives of first through tenth graders, but only 39% of victim narratives by preschoolers, were rated as coherent. When looked at in conjunction with findings concerning the similar contents and foci that victim and perpetrator narratives featured across the various age groups, we are led to conclude that the victim and perpetrator experiences of preschoolers have different qualities (not unlike the victim and perpetrator narratives of older children), but preschoolers' limited ability to integrate aspects of their experience gives *all* of their representations a somewhat choppy and fractured character.

Differences in coherence notwithstanding, the stable nature of the differences between victim and perpetrator narratives across such a broad age range (ages 5–16) is striking. Indeed, given the substantial differences between the narratives of younger and older children, it is noteworthy that across all ages victim narratives differed from perpetrator narratives in similar ways, with narratives given from the victim's perspective featuring, across the ages, a fairly self-referential concern with the harm inflicted and the victim's own emotions, and those given from the perpetrator's perspective featuring a broader concern with the perpetrator's intentions and the victims' emotions and mental states. When preschoolers talked about their own emotions, they, like tenth graders, did so more often when they spoke from the victim's perspective, and when they referred to their own intentions or the other child's emotions they, also like tenth graders, did so more frequently when they spoke from the perpetrator's perspective.

When taken together, these findings suggest that in spite of the divergent ways in which younger and older children seem to experience moral conflicts, the perspective from which they construe their experiences always plays a significant role. Recall, in this regard, that the data discussed here were obtained in a within-subject design, with each child providing one account from the victim's perspective and one from the perpetrator's perspective—a fact that further supports our distinction between age-related differences and perspective differences. Indeed, the fact that older children had a more mature repertoire of psychological knowledge upon which to draw (Astington, 2001; Chandler & Lalonde, 1996; Wellman, 2002) and a better understanding of the viewpoints of those with whom they were in conflict (Flavell, Green, & Flavell, 1986; Gurucharri & Selman, 1982; Selman, 1980) did not eradicate the effect that their specific perspective had on their construals. On the contrary, even as older children drew on their considerable repository of psychological knowledge, their construals still featured distinctly different profiles depending on their position as the victim or the perpetrator. This finding is consistent with findings from attribution research suggesting that even adults exhibit systematic biases in their thinking that are related to their relative perspective (Jones & Nisbett, 1987; Ross & Nisbett, 1991; Ross & Ward, 1996; Pronin et al., 2004). At the other end of the developmental spectrum, young children who had a poorer grasp of the mentalistic elements underlying conflict situations displayed more rudimentary and less coherent construals, which nevertheless also varied in consistent ways with the specific perspective from which they were issued. This finding is consistent with research showing that children as young as 5 make different moral judgments of situations in which they were victims and perpetrators (Smetana et al., 1999) and use different linguistic devices to talk about situations in which they had angered or saddened someone and instances in which someone had angered or saddened them (Bamberg, 2001) or instances in which they were offering or accepting apologies (Sedlak & Walton, 1982).

Recall that a basic assumption guiding our work is that the ways in which children construe, or interpret, their experiences will bear significantly on the moral judgments they make about those experiences. Thus far we have reviewed evidence concerning systematic differences between children's construals from the victim's and the perpetrator's perspectives, as well as systematic differences between younger and older children's construals of their experiences in general. How do these differences become manifested in children's moral judgments? We shall discuss this question at length in the next chapter. Before we do so, as befits a *Monograph* devoted to children's construals of their experiences, we turn to consider, in all their specific and concrete details, examples of narrative construals that younger and older children made about their own experiences from each perspective. In so doing we expect to integrate the findings that we have described thus far in regards to perspective and age differences in narrative content and coherence.

IN CHILDREN'S OWN WORDS

Let us start with the youngest children. The preschoolers' narratives that follow, as was typical of most preschoolers' narratives, are short and do not provide much elaboration but succeed, nonetheless, to capture the specific drama that unfolds, as seen from one perspective or from the other. Both victim and perpetrator narratives, you will notice, are made up largely of behavioral descriptions. Preschool children dwell on little else—there is no landscape of consciousness. The following four accounts (V1–V4) are typical of victim narratives given by preschool children. They capture nicely these children's experiences as targets of aggression. Something was done to me—that seems to be the essence of the victim's perspective. The first two examples, V1 and V2 capture this with just a few words. Whereas examples V3 and V4 contain more details, largely concerning contextual references to time and place, the additional elaboration does not change the substance of their perspective on the unfolding drama.

V1. Um, Jack hit me. And he also, he also kicked me. (Preschool boy)

V2. Um, one time Craig hitted me with his mat. Um, well, he hit me twice. (Preschool girl)

V3. Well, I remember one thing about um someone, um a friend hurting me. I, it was just a little bit. He was a friend, his name was William, he hit me with his hammer in the middle of the head and it really hurt. It was plastic. (Preschool boy)

V4. My friend Sydney, she um she didn't live really close by me, but we have to drive all the way and we go straight and then we turn this way or this way, I don't really know, but then her house is right there at this corner. And um, and um, when I came inside her house, she said she really didn't want to play with me and she um she hit me and um and I felt bad and so I asked her mom, her mom's name is Jana, and I asked Jana if I could go home and she said yes. (Preschool girl)

Next consider, in contrast, the narrative accounts of preschoolers about their experiences as perpetrators. The world as perpetrators see it, even at this young age, is populated by two people: the perpetrator and his or her target. P2, in particular, illustrates the presence of two characters very concretely ("I said . . . he said . . . I said . . . he told me . . . "). In P2 the shift back and forth is smooth; P1 illustrates the incoherence often observed in these accounts. And yet, even though preschoolers' perpetrator narratives are more "heavily populated" than their victim narratives, the people in their narratives, like those in their victim narratives, lack depth. Their narratives include no references to thoughts or beliefs—neither the other child's nor their own. Interestingly, too, for this will change as early as first grade, their perpetrator narratives also omit references to the intentions they presumably had for doing what they did. Read below and see how utterly behavioral preschoolers' construals are. The one exception—noteworthy given the dearth of references to any sort of mental states—is the victim's emotions. Indeed, even as children do not yet speak about their own thoughts, beliefs, or intentions, the other child's emotional responses make an appearance in their perpetrator narratives. As we shall see in the next chapter, when we discuss the moral judgments that young children make about these conflict situations, the victim's plight seems to weigh heavily in the absence of other considerations. Also noteworthy given the attention that the "happy victimizer" phenomenon (Arsenio & Lover, 1999; Arsenio et al., 2006) has received, children do not spontaneously refer to their own emotions as perpetrators (they don't as preschoolers, and they rarely will even as they get older). Instead, it is the victim's emotions that get center stage in the majority of victim narratives, even early on.

> *P1.* I think, I think, um, I think I remember that story when someone was um talking to me and they said, he said, um he said I said um Stephan I don't want to play with you and he was sad. (Preschool boy)

> *P2.* It was today. I was playing with my friend Adam and I said something that really hurt him and he said, "I don't like that." And I stopped. I also pushed him. And I said, "I'm sorry." Because he told me he didn't like it. (Preschool boy)

With age, children's narrative accounts become longer, more detailed, and more elaborated. Instances of physical harm wane, giving way to more psychological forms of harm such as offensive behavior and exclusion. When compared with the narratives given by preschoolers (even those that included more detail), the following two narratives given by first grade children illustrate how, by the age of about 6, children's construals begin to acquire a "landscape of consciousness" (something which will be of consequence to their moral judgments). As shown in V5, victims will continue to focus on the harm inflicted on them, often reiterating and emphasizing this element in their narratives; references to their own emotions now make an appearance, to remain thereafter a staple—indeed, a defining element—of victim narratives. Perpetrators, as illustrated by P3, will continue attending to the victim's emotional responses, but will also begin considering their own goals and intentions; their own emotions, on the other hand, will remain largely unmentioned. This shift into considering the mental life (thoughts, wants, goals) of two people will become a hallmark of perpetrator narratives. P3 below illustrates one of the ways in which this happens: competing goals and desires will embody much of the conflict as experienced by perpetrators. This too will be of consequence to their moral judgments.

> *V5.* One time at Jo's birthday party like last year, she invited me to her new house and she's all like "you're my best friend" but then but then she said it

to another boy, but I don't know him. I just know that she said it to him because I watched her and it kind of hurt my feelings and it made me feel uncomfortable then too. Well, um it was night time when I came home from her birthday party. And, and I kind of thought to myself that was kind of making me feel bad. So I wonder if I can go over there and tell her that that kind of hurt my feelings—so that's what I want to do someday because I still can't get it out of my mind. She's a best friend of mine and I just can't get it out of my mind because she, because, because whenever I walked home from her house at night time she would always give me a hug and I would always do that and we would and I would never want to leave her house. Then at the birthday, but I'm still kind of wondering if she said it, I'm wondering if he's really her um best friend. She is one of my very, very best friends. She's the best out of all of them. (First grade girl)

P3. This wasn't really a bad disagreement, but once my friend like wanted to like paint, because she always likes to paint. And sometimes I'll do it, but I don't really like to because it's not one of my favorite things, and also she always does it, so, I get bored of it. So, um, once I sort of just like, "No, I don't want to do it," and so um, she's like, "Fine, then I'm going home." So we got in a huge disagreement, but I know she could go home because um, her house was just across the street, and I didn't want her to go home, but I really didn't want to paint, so I was like, "What should I do, what should I do?" And so I just said, "Okay, we'll paint, I'm sorry." (First grade girl)

What distinguishes the narratives of fifth and tenth graders from those of first graders is not so much the level of detail and elaboration but the sense one gets that these older children recognize (even if implicitly) that some of what is happening is actually taking place internally, in their own and in the other child's minds. So whereas a first grader was able to capture nicely the interaction between the two parties, with their distinct goals or desires, as in P3's statement, "I sort of just like, 'No, I don't want to do it,' and so um, she's like, 'Fine, then I'm going home,'" older children (see P4–P6) let us know how the two parties have different thoughts, goals, or construals of what is going on (e.g., "Arial just couldn't know that, that I felt that way, right?", "I guess she just wanted me to take her side.," "I'm pretty sure she understood what I meant," "I'm sure she was expecting I would . . . ," "I bet she felt betrayed," "Maybe even she thought I don't care about her"). Because older children can do this, it is noteworthy that they do not do it to the same extent in their victim narratives as they do in their perpetrator narratives.

When children speak from the victim's perspective, whatever the other child may have thought or meant, or even felt, is given little consideration. In this respect, the first two victim narratives below (V6 and V7) are not that different from the victim narratives given by younger children. In the next chapter we will discuss how the self-referential focus of victim narratives becomes manifested in their moral judgments. Here we also speculate that victims' failure to consider the other party's thoughts, goals, and intentions may also underlie what seem like fairly primitive responses and approaches to conflict resolution. The narrative of V6, in particular, is a concrete example of how, by not considering what the perpetrator's goals, intentions, or possible construal of the situation may have been, V6 locked himself into a nonresolution. This is not to say that if victims were to consider both sides of the conflict they would not feel hurt. As shown in V8, tenth graders did sometimes, as victims, ponder the perpetrator's construal or goals (e.g., maybe his friend refused him a ride because "more of the other guys that he didn't hang out with very much are showing interest because he now has a car and he can drive around") but still felt hurt by the perpetrator's actions. It may be, and this remains to be seen when we talk about children's moral judgments, that in those cases in which victims do consider the perpetrator's experience, their moral judgments about the perpetrator's actions are less harsh and categorical.

> *V6.* Well, my uh other best friend, I have two, and um so uh he's a really skate board fanatic and this new kid moved in and all he did was hang out with that kid for so long, and I just felt like I was being really left out. And so he asked me to uh come over one day and I'm all happy, and then that kid shows up and then he just like completely leaves me and goes with him, and I'm just really feeling left out and I get aggravated and I get pretty angry and I uh lose my temper and I just kind of leave without saying goodbye and all, take my bike out of there and um what really made me angry is that he didn't like care that I went, all he was doing was playing with that kid. And so I just hated it, and I wasn't feeling too good about that kid either. So he called me up again and so I really turned him down, I just hung up and then uh we didn't talk to each other for a long time after that. And well finally one day he just kind of showed up and I saw him and I was still really ticked off that he'd just ditched me and gone with that other kid. And so I just closed the door and a few minutes later he knocked on it and he looked really, really sad and said that he was really sorry and all. (Fifth grade boy)

> *V7.* Um last year, we, I'm a dancer and I dance all the time and I cheerlead, but we were doing this thing that we do at our homecoming half-time dance. It's called the bulldog boogie. And we get all the little kids from all the other schools, and they can come sign up and they dance with their age group at half-time. And I was leading it last year. It was my freshmen year. And we wore um, like spandex capris and then this top that was like to here. And one of my other friends, they started talking about me and saying that I was

fat to all these little kids around. And I was so upset, like, I started crying. I was so upset. And, um, one of my friends came up to me and asked me what was wrong. And I just started bawling and my friend was, and I said, "Just because they have perfect bodies and they don't have anything to complain about, doesn't mean that they need to be talking bad about me or anybody else, that has, that has fat on their body." And so that was not a good situation. (Tenth grade girl)

V8. Um, my friend can drive and we, we, all us teenage boys like to go ride around with our friends and have fun. And I didn't want to just go cruise around, I asked him for a ride to a place that I needed to be for an appointment and he was pretty much the only ride I could get without walking, and I didn't want to walk, so I asked him and he said that was alright. So the next day he, I saw him in the morning and said, "Is the ride still okay?" And he said yeah, and we went through the day and about an hour before the day ended he was going up to one of his classes and I noticed he had his jacket and his keys and all the stuff he usually has when he just takes off from school. And I thought about it and thought, "maybe he's just gonna take off without me." So, I thought about it and stayed there, and tried to find another ride, but I couldn't, so at the end of the day before he could get to his car, I ran down to his car to meet him. And he showed up a little while later with other kids and I asked him, "Can I still have a ride?" and he said, "Oh, no." And I begged and begged and he finally said okay. So, he gave me a ride, but he talked to the other guys more than he usually talks to me, so I was kind of wondering what was going on, so I asked him, and he said, "Nothing." I think it's because more of the other guys that he didn't hang out with very much are showing interest because he now has a car and he can drive around. He has a nice car and everyone wants his car, and everything. He dropped me off and I, before I could say thanks, he kind of took off, so, and I felt kind of bad. (Tenth grade boy)

Compare the victim construals above with those that children the same age made from the perpetrator's perspective (P4–P6). Recall that victim and perpetrator narratives were not different in their length, amount of detail, or elaboration. Rather, the same amount of detail and elaboration was used, as it were, for a different purpose. P4, for example, tells us not only what (in her view) happened between her and her friend and what, in her view, her friend felt; she also relates what she thought her friend's perspective on the situation may have been—what her friend may have wanted, what she may or may not have known, and what she may or may not have understood. In saying that perpetrators attend to both sides of the conflict we do not mean that perpetrators are "better," nicer, or more caring than their victims. All three narratives from the perpetrator's perspective below show this not to be the case. Our point, rather, is that the perpetrator's perspective on the conflict situation includes more than their own experience. This dual attention to the two sides of the conflict situation—their own goals and the other child's—will be of substantial importance to moral judgments.

P4. Um, well this is a little thing about Shelly too, but it's mostly about my friend Jess. She's a really nice girl, she's really cool. And I like her. And at recess one day, my friends and I were in a circle, and just talking and stuff. And Shelly was one of the people in the circle and so was Jess. And um Jess was um Jess like Shelly pushed Jess out of the circle but I didn't see, and then Jess, told me. She like took me out of the circle and stuff and um she said, "Well Shelly just pushed me out of the circle." And, ok, everyone tells me their problems, and I'm like the problem solver in the class. And I hate it. I absolutely hate it. At my old school, it was like that and everything. I hate it. So I just said "yes that's nice" and then I went away, but then I kind of felt bad because I wish I would have explained it a little better to her uh I'm not the problem solver in the class, I'm just like a normal kid like everyone else, I hate it. Uh, but Jess just couldn't know that, that I felt that way, right? I guess she just wanted me to take her side and so she was uh kind of hurt feelings, but she wasn't mad at me, and uh I'm pretty sure she understood what I meant but still I'm not sure. Yeah. But I really wish I would have explained it a little better because I like can't be solving everyone's problems but it's not like I don't like her and I hate getting in fights. I hate it. (Fifth grade girl)

P5. 'I remember this uh was just a few months ago I remember I was supposed to, one of my best friends uh I was supposed to hang out with her one night and I really didn't want to and I ended up, I wanted to go with somebody else and the person that I wanted to go with had another friend that they weren't friends really, and so it uh was kind of hard to split up time and whatnot. So I remember I uh told her I would go with her one night and uh so I'm sure she was expecting I would, and I kind of said I would knowing that I couldn't and I had already made previous plans. And I remember uh I kind of lied to her but I mostly like avoided her one night and avoided like phone calls, and she must've been expecting to do something, I bet she was like waiting by the phone waiting for me to call, and then she figured it out and found out and she felt really bad and was hurt and so it wasn't good. 'Cause I bet she felt betrayed, maybe even she thought I don't care about her but I do, I didn't want to hurt her feelings because she was one of my best friends and so I know sometimes being honest is hard but it would definitely be worth it, but it was hard just because I felt so pressured like it happens a lot I know it happens to a lot to people my age especially, that you feel so pressured that you want to do something with one person but then you promised to another person, and uh I don't know, you want to be everywhere and you want to be everyone's friend and you don't want to hurt anybody but you also really just want to do what feels good, and that definitely was part of the situation. I wanted her to feel okay. But I mean she got over it we're friends and everything. (Tenth grade girl)

P6. Okay, well, this guy, his name's Dave. Um, last year uh um I asked him to Winters, but I just thought we were going to go as friends and he took it the totally wrong way. And everyone said, "Yeah, he really likes you." And I said, "Oh stop. He does not," you know. And then uh everyone said, "You have to tell him that you just want to be friends with him." And I didn't, and I kept not doing it. And like, and then the night came and he wanted to ask me out, and I said, "Don't. I don't want to go out with you," and I was really mean and I like pushed him. I was just really off. And so, he just said, "Okay, I'm just going to go. I just uh can't do this anymore. You're really being annoying." He used stronger words, but we won't use those. And um, so then the next week he was so sad. He would uh he was friends with my best friend, her name is Julia, and so uh I know that I really hurt him and I like made him cry because I was just, uh put out all the wrong messages and I did all these things that I shouldn't have done, and anyways. And so he thought it all meant something else and he had a different idea. Um, I was just really horrible, y'know, I just wasn't nice, like I should be to him . . . So uh, well so I just had to tell him, I just had to because we were just having a good time together and I didn't want to be serious or anything, so uh, but he was so upset by that, he just wanted y'know something else and so like there was no way out, no good way out. And so it took a long time to build things back. Yeah. (Tenth grade girl)

When compared with the fairly smooth telling in their victim narratives, the perpetrator narratives given by fifth and tenth graders also illustrate the many false starts and dysfluencies that crop up as children focus on both sides of the event. Finally, P4–P6 also serve to illustrate the sorts of intentions depicted most often by older perpetrators. P4's actions were, in her telling, not deliberate. They seemed, rather, impulsive, an outburst in response to what she perceived to be her friend's unreasonable demands or expectations. It is not hard to imagine how P4's victim (Jess) may have construed the situation—being so inexplicably let down by a friend. P4 notes her friend's dismay and distress, but her own history and her own needs (to be treated as a "normal kid," not a problem solver) are also fully present in her telling. The fact that the behavior was an outburst is not construed by P4 as meaning she was not responsible for her friend's distress, and she keeps wishing she had explained herself better thus avoiding "a fight." The actions of P5 and P6 have a more deliberate feel to them.

60

P5 acknowledges lying to her friend for a self-serving reason. And yet, P5 also says that she did not want to betray her friend's trust; what she wanted was to spend time with a different friend—a goal which is not intrinsically hurtful or immoral. After some hesitation, P6 first was deliberate in putting a stop to her friend's unrequited romantic advances even as she was aware that would cause him pain. Her reason was "selfish," but not illegitimate: the choice to date someone is quintessentially personal. Together, the perpetrator narratives by P4, P5, and P6 capture the sort of "not-quite-intentional-but-not-quite-unintentional" world of harm that children seem to inhabit. We shall have more to say about this shortly.

Even as we underscore the distinct ways in which children of different ages construe situations in which they were victims or perpetrators, we must also underscore that all narratives had one important feature in common. Preschoolers and tenth graders alike spoke not about rules or commands, and did not refer to what they "have to do" or what they were taught to do. Their construals of situations of moral conflict and transgression convey moments of interpersonal interactions and interpersonal communications in which one person's actions injure another. Children describe persons engaging in mean or inconsiderate behaviors, persons expressing distress and anger and, sometimes, persons making amends. They also convey how children, during the interactions, perceive and consider the consequences that those actions had on them and others, and often debate what they should do. These elements, we argue, are what moral judgments are made of.

V. MORAL JUDGMENTS ABOUT CONFLICTS AS UNDERSTOOD

There is a wealth of research evidence indicating that children bring their moral concepts to bear on situations in which one person harms or mistreats another. Children do so in regards to hypothetical conflict situations (Smetana, 2006; Turiel, 1998) and in regards to actual conflict situations that were observed in their classrooms and playgrounds (Smetana et al., 1999; Turiel, 2005). Hence it is not surprising that children bring their moral concepts to bear on conflict situations in which they were directly involved as victims and perpetrators. Indeed, it would have been surprising had they not done so. And yet, unlike hypothetical situations or even situations arising among others they know, in this study we considered those situations in which the children themselves were those who behaved aggressively or unfairly toward others, or the direct targets of their friends' and peers' aggressive or unfair actions. As we stated at the outset, packed into these situations is an unyielding tension between moral judgment and moral behavior. How do children integrate their judgment that it is wrong to inflict harm on others with the experience of having hurt someone or having been hurt by someone?

With this broad question in mind, we consider the data on the moral judgments which children, at different ages, made of their own transgressions and of those transgressions of which they became victims (see Table 13). Generally speaking, across perspectives and ages, the majority of children (71%) thought that the perpetrator's actions depicted in their narratives were wrong. However, significant differences were found in the evaluations given from each perspective. On average, the perpetrators' actions were judged more negatively from the victim's than from the perpetrator's perspective, $F(1, 108) = 18.84$, $p < .001$, $\eta^2 = .15$.

As shown in Table 13, the large majority of children (85%) judged the perpetrator's behavior negatively when speaking from the perspective of the victim, but their evaluations were more varied when they spoke from the perpetrator's perspective, with nearly half of them (43%) evaluating at

TABLE 13

MEAN EVALUATIONS, AND PROPORTIONS OF POSITIVE, MIXED, AND NEGATIVE EVALUATIONS,
BY AGE AND PERSPECTIVE

| | Age and Perspective | | | | | | | |
| | Victim | | | | Perpetrator | | | |
	Preschool	First Grade	Fifth Grade	Tenth Grade	Preschool	First Grade	Fifth Grade	Tenth Grade
M evaluations	2.8	2.9	2.6	2.7	2.3	2.2	2.6	2.3
(*SD*)	(0.5)	(0.4)	(0.7)	(0.4)	(0.9)	(0.9)	(0.7)	(0.8)
Positive evaluations	.07	.04	.14	.04	.29	.25	.11	.11
(*SD*)	(.26)	(.19)	(.36)	(.19)	(.46)	(.44)	(.31)	(.31)
Mixed evaluations	.04$_a$	.00$_a$	.07$_a$	.21$_b$	.11$_a$	.21$_a$	.18$_a$	.46$_b$
(*SD*)	(.19)	(.00)	(.26)	(.42)	(.31)	(.42)	(.39)	(.51)
Negative evaluations	.89	.96	.79	.75	.61	.54	.71	.43
(*SD*)	(.31)	(.19)	(.42)	(.44)	(.50)	(.51)	(.46)	(.50)

Note.—Means range from 1 ("okay") to 3 ("not okay"). Mean proportions in the same row (within the same perspective) that do not share subscripts differ at $p < .05$ in Duncan multiple-range tests. Mean proportions of evaluation types may not add up to 1.00 because of rounding.

least some aspects of their own actions (as perpetrators) as acceptable. In our interpretation, differences in children's moral judgments are tied to differences in construals. The design of the present study does not allow us to draw direct connections between a specific construal and a specific judgment. Unlike the research we have conducted in the past with hypothetical stimuli (Wainryb, 1991, 1993; Wainryb et al., 1998), the present study did not include a set of standardized experiences but, rather, a large variety of unique experiences with unique construals which cannot be manipulated in a controlled fashion along specific dimensions. Nevertheless, in interpreting the differences between the moral judgments that children made from each perspective, we were guided by the findings concerning the distinct ways in which children construe their victim and perpetrator experiences. For, if the notion of construal is taken seriously, it may be said that victims and perpetrators were evaluating different objects of judgment, or different realities. (To some extent this is also true of younger vs. older children. We will further discuss age differences later in this chapter.)

When children had been the victims, their construals of the conflict situations focused largely on their own experience. Their nearly unanimous negative evaluations of these incidents, evaluations which they grounded on the pain and distress they had suffered, are consistent with this unique focus. The justifications given by victims for their judgments (see Table 14) further support this point. Indeed the large majority of victims (71%) referred to the harm or injustice inflicted on the victim.

TABLE 14

TYPES OF JUSTIFICATIONS, BY PERSPECTIVE (PROPORTIONS)

	Perspective	
Justifications	Victim	Perpetrator
Harm	.55	.47
(SD)	(.50)	(.50)
Justice	.16$_a$	.07$_b$
(SD)	(.37)	(.26)
Personal goals	.01$_a$	.08$_b$
(SD)	(.09)	(.27)
Necessary harm	.06$_a$	.13$_b$
(SD)	(.19)	(.33)
Competing desires	.04	.09
(SD)	(.19)	(.29)
No intent to harm	.05	.05
(SD)	(.21)	(.21)
Rules and authority	.10	.05
(SD)	(.30)	(.23)
Unelaborated	.06	.06
(SD)	(.24)	(.24)

Note.—Mean proportions in the same row that do not share subscripts differ at $p < .05$ in follow-up ANOVAs with perspective as a repeated measure. Mean proportions may not add up to 1.00 because of rounding.

When *the same children* spoke about incidents in which they had been the perpetrators, they too attended to the victim's experience. Indeed, by furnishing narratives in response to our request to tell us "about a time when you did or said something and a friend or a child you know well ended up feeling hurt by it," all children had implicitly acknowledged having had some role in the other child's distress. Beyond that, the majority also referred explicitly, in their narratives, to the victims' feelings and distress. Nevertheless, in addition to attending to the victims' experience, perpetrators included in their narratives references to elements of their own experiences—their own thoughts, goals, desires, and intentions. We suggest that the dual focus of perpetrators' construals may be associated with their diverse (as opposed to the victims' uniformly negative) judgments.

In some cases, aspects of the experience of one or the other person appear to weigh more heavily. If the victim's plight weighs more heavily in the perpetrators' eyes, they are likely to judge their own actions negatively. For example,

DO YOU THINK IT WAS OKAY OR NOT OKAY FOR YOU TO CALL HIM A WUSS? Well, I was really just trying to get him to come paint-balling with us, but I don't think it was okay 'cause it was pretty mean and it really hurt his feelings.

Overall, 57% of children (speaking from the perpetrator's perspective) weighed the victim's plight more heavily and judged their own actions negatively (as compared with 85% when speaking from the victim's perspective, $F(1, 108) = 24.05$, $p < .001$, $\eta^2 = .18$). When aspects of their own experience weigh more heavily, perpetrators might judge their actions as being justified; 19% made this type of judgment, as compared with 7% when speaking from the victim's perspective, $F(1, 108) = 7.32$, $p = .008$, $\eta^2 = .06$. In this case, perpetrators referred to their own personal goals or preferences as means for justifying why their behavior had not been wrong; in their view, the legitimacy of their own goals justified their acts (only 1% of victims invoked this type of reasoning, $F(1, 107) = 8.39$, $p = .005$, $\eta^2 = .07$). The following examples illustrate this kind of reasoning.

DO YOU THINK IT WAS OKAY OR NOT OKAY THAT YOU DIDN'T LET BECKA PLAY TAG WITH YOU? It wasn't wrong that I didn't let her play because I wanted to be *it*.

DO YOU THINK IT WAS OKAY OR NOT OKAY THAT YOU TOLD ALEX HE COULDN'T BE ON YOUR TEAM? It was okay that we told him he couldn't be on our team, because we didn't want to be on a bad team.

DO YOU THINK IT WAS OKAY OR NOT OKAY FOR YOU TO TELL CANDICE SHE COULDN'T PLAY WITH YOU? Well, I guess we kinda knew that she'd feel sad because of that, but all we wanted to do was to play alone. That's not wrong.

DO YOU THINK IT WAS OKAY OR NOT OKAY FOR YOU TO TELL KATIE THAT YOU DIDN'T WANT TO GO OUT WITH HER? It was totally fine, because, y'know, I didn't want to go out with her. If I hadn't told her, then I probably would have ended up going out with her for like a month, and it would have been a waste of a month.

In other cases, elements of both the victim's experience and the perpetrator's experience appear to weigh heavily in perpetrators' eyes. It appears as though children resist suppressing or subordinating their own goals to avoid causing distress to someone else, but the perceived legitimacy of their goals does not insulate them from worrying about the victim's distress or from their guilt about having caused that distress. When conflict situations are construed in this way, perpetrators are likely to make judgments that are at once both positive and negative (24% made mixed evaluations of this type when speaking from the perpetrator's perspective, as compared with only 8% from the victim's perspective, $F(1, 108) = 13.89$,

$p < .001, \eta^2 = .11$). This type of mixed evaluation was grounded on two types of justifications. In one, which we labeled "necessary harm" (but could have labeled, more dramatically, "necessary evil"), children reasoned that while they had acted in ways that were harsh or painful for the victim, their actions in and of themselves had been legitimate and even necessary, as when children confronted a friend concerning an unacceptable behavior either to protect the friend or the relationship. The following examples illustrate this type of reasoning (a portion of the narrative precedes some of the examples of moral judgments, for clarity):

> Um, in second grade, um my friend Erin, we, uh, were really, really good friends in first grade and um, I said uh, one day she was doing her work and stuff and I thought she had the wrong answer, and so I said, "That's the wrong answer," and stuff, and so she got kind of offensed [sic] by that, because I think I didn't say it nicely enough. But I was just trying to help her get the right answer. And um, then it kind of turned into this big fight and then she said some mean things and it hurt both of us really bad. ... DO YOU THINK IT WAS OKAY OR NOT OKAY FOR YOU TO TELL ERIN THAT THE PROBLEMS ON HER PAPER WERE WRONG? Well I don't think it was okay *how* I said that, but it was okay *that* I said that. Because she *had* the wrong answers but, well, I guess I should think more about what I'm going to say before I actually say it. And I really think about that. And I said it a wrong way than I should have said it. And I said it kind of mean and it hurt her feelings, but I didn't really know how I said it.

> I guess William was getting on my nerves a little bit. His views were pissing me off about something and ... and I told him off, I can't remember what I said, but I told him off, and it totally devastated him. And like we uh we were in recess or P.E. and he just left, he went back in the classroom. DO YOU THINK IT WAS OKAY OR NOT OKAY FOR YOU TELL WILLIAM OFF? Probably shouldn't have told him off, because it really upset him, but I think if I hadn't told him off, his continuing, his continually, his constant complaining would have broken off our relationship. So I think it needed to be done.

This type of reason was given more often by perpetrators than by victims, $F(1, 107) = 7.84$, $p = .006$, $\eta^2 = .07$. In a slightly different argument ("competing desires"), children recognized that the pursuit of their own goals would necessarily thwart the other child's goals and unavoidably result in distress for that child. Tenth graders often resorted to this reasoning in regards to incidents that involved a decision to break up a romantic attachment, and young children referred to competing desires in regards to conflicting preferences for games or activities. The following examples illustrate this type of reasoning:

DO YOU THINK IT WAS OKAY OR NOT OKAY FOR YOU TO NOT LET JORDAN PLAY WITH THE BIONICLES? I don't think it was okay, it was not okay, but I just didn't have enough stuff [i.e., "Bionicles"]. SO WHY WAS IT NOT OKAY? Because she was just being left out and I was just playing with my friend and my brother. She might feel sad and it's not right. But the choice was to leave her out or destroy my game because we couldn't play if she played too.

DO YOU THINK THAT IS WAS OKAY OR NOT OKAY FOR YOU TO TELL EMILY THAT YOU WANTED TO PLAY ANIMALS INSTEAD OF BARBIES? I didn't really feel like telling her, but I wanted to play animals so I had to tell her what I want to play. SO DO YOU THINK IT WAS OKAY OR NOT OKAY FOR YOU TO TELL HER THAT? Not really okay because I didn't want to hurt her feelings, but I had to tell her because I wanted to play animals.

DO YOU THINK IT WAS OKAY OR NOT OKAY FOR YOU TO TELL ANGIE THAT YOU STILL LIKED YOUR EX-GIRLFRIEND? Um, I really don't know. Right then I would have said it's not okay, she was so upset, but looking back on it, it's okay that I told her instead of going on and on, but all in all, I think it was okay to tell her and, um, get it out there. Get it in the open. If she accepted it, she accepted. If she didn't like it, she didn't like it. I mean it wasn't alright that I told her, like when she cried, but it was still okay that I told her because I also still had feelings, like, I still kind of wanted to be with my ex.

That children make varied moral judgments when considering situations that pit two concerns against one another is not new to the field of moral development research. Findings from multiple studies using Kohlberg's hypothetical dilemmas (Kohlberg, 1969), pro-social dilemmas (Eisenberg, 1989; Eisenberg & Mussen, 1989), and mixed-domain events (common among researchers from the domains perspective; Helwig, 2006; Killen et al., 2002; Neff, Turiel, & Anshel, 2002; Smetana et al., 1991) have reliably indicated that, in response to such mixed situations, children might give priority to one or the other concern or might attempt to coordinate both concerns. Research using events that comprise overlapping moral and non-moral considerations has, furthermore, shown that children's judgments shift fairly systematically when the relative salience of each component is experimentally manipulated (e.g., Helwig, 2006; Killen et al., 2002; Smetana et al., 1991).

Our findings, that children made diverse judgments (sometimes positive, sometimes negative, and sometimes mixed) about their construals of perpetrator events are therefore consistent with previous moral development research, inasmuch as perpetrators' construals tended to pit the victim's experience against the perpetrator's. The further contribution of our research lies in showing that children actually construe their own conflict experiences as mixed, but do so in regards to situations in which they were involved as perpetrators but not so much in those in which they were involved as victims. The dual-focus of the construals of perpetrators and the self-referential focus of the construals of victims, we propose, are at the basis of their differing moral judgments.

To argue, as we have in this chapter, that children's moral judgments can be understood in relation to their own construals of conflict situations raises a hoard of concerns with motivational forces that, consciously or not, may operate in ways that bias or distort their judgments, their construals, or both. Before we concern ourselves with these issues, we turn to reviewing the age differences we have observed in children's moral judgments.

AGE DIFFERENCES IN MORAL JUDGMENTS

Whereas mean evaluations did not vary by age, a MANOVA on the proportions of positive, mixed, and negative evaluations yielded a significant age effect, $F(6, 216) = 2.89$, $p = .010$, $\eta^2 = .07$, with older children making more mixed evaluations than younger ones, $F(3, 108) = 6.02$, $p = .001$, $\eta^2 = .14$. This effect is more immediately noticeable in regards to the evaluations made from the perpetrator's perspective, where 11% of preschoolers, as compared with about 20% of first and fifth graders and 46% of tenth graders, made mixed evaluations, $F(3, 108) = 3.95$, $p = .010$, $\eta^2 = .10$. The MANOVA on the justifications also yielded a significant effect of age, $F(21, 309) = 2.00$, $p = .006$, $\eta^2 = .12$, with older children offering more mixed justifications than younger children. In particular, tenth graders more so than any other age group, $F(3, 107) = 8.65$, $p < .001$, $\eta^2 = .20$, referred to "necessary harm."

The finding that young children made fewer mixed judgments than their older peers is consistent with findings from the moral development literature (e.g., Helwig, 2006; Killen et al., 2002; Shaw & Wainryb, 2005) showing that younger children tend to make more categorical moral judgments. This effect has been said to be, at least in part, due to younger children's lesser ability to, for example, simultaneously consider more than one element of a complex situation (e.g., Harter & Whitesell, 1989; Helwig, 2006; Killen et al., 2002; Smetana et al., 1991; Shaw & Wainryb, 2005). We have argued, further, that their lesser ability to consider psychological aspects as they construe their understanding of social situations may also be implicated in their categorical moral judgments (Wainryb & Brehl, in press).

Recall that preschoolers' narrative construals seldom included references to the psychological aspects of experience, namely, intentions, thoughts, and emotions, and those of first graders included references to mostly desires and preferences. We have already suggested (in Chapter IV) that the scarce references to psychological elements in young children's narratives is consistent with their constrained psychological understandings (e.g., Astington et al., 1988; Bartsch & Wellman, 1995; Lalonde & Chandler, 2002; Wellman, 2002)—why would preschoolers bother referring to their own or the other child's intentions or beliefs about the situation if such information would by necessity mirror the information they do give about actions and their outcomes? Now we consider how those features might become implicated in their categorical moral thinking.

In our view (see also Wainryb & Brehl, in press), behind young children's impoverished understanding of the psychological dimensions of a conflict situation lies a tendency to conflate mental states and outcomes. Take, as an example, children's understandings of intentions. It has been documented that young children tend to conflate intentions and outcomes and thus assume that actors had intended whatever outcomes came about (Astington, 2001; Kalish, 2005; Piaget, 1932). Young children's tendency to over-attribute intentionality and make categorical (negative) moral judgments about incidents that resulted in harm merely follows from their assumption about "how things are." Older children, on the other hand, who have developed an understanding of intention as a mental state distinct from action, should be more likely to refer to an actor's intention as separate from his/her behavior. What matters, however, is not that older children refer more often, in their narratives, to intentions, but rather that in doing so they are manifesting their belief or understanding that the outcome of someone's actions may be different from whatever that person may have intended. Consider for comparison the following two judgments of a situation in which the narrator had excluded a peer from a desirable activity:

DO YOU THINK IT WAS OKAY OR NOT OKAY FOR YOU TO LEAVE DANNY OUT? It was just not okay to leave him out because it made him feel not so good.

DO YOU THINK IT WAS OKAY OR NOT OKAY FOR YOU TO LEAVE SARAH OUT? It was kind of okay and also kind of not okay, because I wasn't trying to hurt her feelings when I didn't invite her to come over, I was really just trying to get to know another group of people, but still she did get hurt.

Younger children's limited ability to conceive of situations in which the outcome of an act may have been in conflict with, or unrelated to, a stated intention explains the first example above, of a categorically negative moral judgment. Young children's non-representational understandings of beliefs (e.g., Chandler & Lalonde, 1996; Lalonde & Chandler, 2002) and emotions (especially mixed emotions; Gnepp & Klayman, 1992; Harris, 1989; Harter & Whitesell, 1989), have been shown to contribute in similar ways to impoverished construals and categorical moral judgments (see Wainryb & Ford, 1998; Wainryb & Brehl, in press). The second example, of a mixed evaluation made about a similar sort of situation, illustrates how an older child can distinguish between intentional behavior (i.e., behavior that is not accidental) and the intention behind such behavior and, while acknowledging that the behavior discussed was not accidental and that the outcome of such behavior was harmful, also recognizes that there had been no intent to inflict harm. (Recall that in the previous chapter we had suggested that in cases in which victims consider the perpetrator's intentions and goals, such as the example of V8, their moral judgments of the perpetrator's actions might be less harsh and categorical).

From the start our argument has been that different construals of interpersonal conflicts would be associated with differences in moral judgment. In this section we suggest that age differences in children's construals of their conflict experiences (largely associated with less and more elaborated understandings of the psychological elements of conflict situations) may be associated with the age differences we have observed in children's moral judgments. Are we thus suggesting that development happens not in the moral domain but elsewhere? Are we perhaps suggesting that development in the moral domain depends on development in other domains? The short answer is, "no." The fuller answer, one that also addresses just what we think does develop, is longer and less categorical.

We take a constructivist and interactional perspective on moral development (Turiel, 1983, 1998, 2002). Children develop moral concepts and understandings by abstracting and reflecting on features of social interactions that bear on harm and justice. Children's construals of situations surrounding moral conflict serve to illustrate this process well. Recall our discussion, in the previous chapter, of the features that make up children's construals—actions, communications, observations, and reflections. It is out of these elements that children's moral development emerges. Although conceptual changes in children's moral understandings do not depend on children's interpretations of their social interactions, these interpretations constitute the context within which both social interactions and conceptual changes happen. Complex and nuanced interpretations of social reality and interpersonal conflict are likely to offer a different context for conceptual change than simpler ones.

Indeed, even as moral development does not depend upon children's varying construals of reality, the two are inextricably intertwined in children's experiences. This has important implications for the interpretation of age differences in moral thinking and, more broadly, for the study of the development of moral concepts. In this study, for example, we have observed age differences in children's moral judgments. In our view, it would be a mistake to interpret these differences as reflecting solely differences in moral concepts. We have tried to make a case for the proposition that these differences are related to differences in the ways younger and older children construe, interpret, and make sense of such situations. We will not say—for we do not know—whether their moral concepts are also different. Our study cannot answer such a question, largely because to determine that differences in judgments reflect differences in moral concepts it must, first, be determined that children of all ages have a shared understanding of the situations they are making judgments about. While it may be feasible to accomplish this within the context of laboratory research, the task becomes much more complicated for those interested in understanding children's actual experiences with moral conflict and transgression. We do not rule out that younger children in this study not only construed situations differently but also brought to bear on these construals simpler moral concepts. More importantly, our proposition concerning the relation between construals and judgments does not, in any way, rule out development in the moral domain. We do propose, however, that a fundamental challenge of researchers intent on charting children's moral development is to distinguish between the complexity in children's moral concepts and the complexity of their construals and understandings of the background against which such concepts are applied.

VI. MORAL CONFLICTS, SUBJECTIVITY, AND DEVELOPMENT

The research reported in this *Monograph* documents the narrative accounts and moral evaluations that children, across a broad age range, made of their own interpersonal conflicts with peers. A noteworthy feature of these data was that children rarely chose to describe incidents that had happened the same day or the day before; rather, they seemed to reach back to events that were memorable to them. Moreover, with minimal probing, children eagerly provided accounts not only of incidents in which they had been the targets of their peers' unfair or harmful actions but also of incidents in which they had been those mistreating or inflicting harm on others. The ease with which they recalled those situations and the richness of their descriptions strongly suggest that interpersonal harm, concerns with their own and others' welfare, and moral thinking are an important part of children's social lives. The multiple analyses carried out on both their narrative construals and moral judgments suggested, furthermore, that situations of moral conflict are understood and evaluated differently by victims and perpetrators.

In discussing the meaning of these differences it is important to bear in mind how these data were obtained. Recall that, in this study, each child provided one account from the victim's perspective and one from the perpetrator's perspective. The strategy of having each child furnish both victim and perpetrator accounts is essential for interpreting the results because it rules out the possibility that victims and perpetrators were different kinds of children, thereby allowing us to interpret the observed differences between victims' and perpetrators' accounts and judgments as being associated with differences in perspective. Nonetheless, two concerns may be raised in regards to this research strategy.

One potential concern is that because victim narratives and perpetrator narratives do not refer to the same incident, the accuracy or truthfulness of children's accounts cannot be verified. Although this is a limitation of the research strategy employed, alternative methodologies cannot completely eliminate the concern with the accuracy and truthfulness of children's

accounts. For example, even if both accounts—the victim's and the perpetrator's—were to refer to the same incident, the question of who, if anyone,
was telling the truth would nonetheless persist. Similarly, comparing children's victim and perpetrator construals with observations of their actual
behavior would also not eliminate the concern with accuracy, as it cannot be
assumed that adult observers are necessarily more accurate than the children involved in the conflict (especially as children, but not adult observers,
may be privy to aspects of their past interactions that give meanings to their
current conflicts; see Shantz, 1993). More importantly, this limitation does
not seriously hamper the interpretation of our findings because the purpose
of this study was not to establish how accurately victims and perpetrators
accounted for what happened, but rather to document the systematic ways
in which they construed what happened. This is not to say that accuracy or
truthfulness are not important or that children's narrative accounts are
mere fabrication or fiction (more about this below), but rather that the main
questions of this study bear on children's interpretation of their experience.

Another concern that may be raised about our procedures refers to the
fact that each child furnished a victim account of one event and a perpetrator account of a different event. It is possible that when children think
about themselves as victims they choose to relate more severe incidents or
incidents in which, for example, the perpetrator acted with the intention to
hurt them. Conversely, it may be that when children think about themselves
as perpetrators they tell about less severe incidents, or incidents in which
their behaviors were clearly justified or mitigated by circumstances. Although it is impossible to determine with certainty that none of the differences observed between victim and perpetrator narratives arose from
children's choice of which victim and perpetrator conflict situations to describe in the first place, our findings indicate that there were few differences
between the victim and perpetrator narratives in the types of harm depicted. From both the victim's and perpetrator's perspectives, children depicted
incidents about offensive behavior, exclusion and physical harm; from both
perspectives, too, children depicted incidents that entailed a similar mag-
nitude of harm. (We also examined the possibilities that children might have
furnished a second narrative much longer or shorter than the first, or that
the order in which victim and perpetrator narratives were elicited had an
effect on children's construals and evaluations; no sequence or order effects
were found.) Furthermore, very few children when speaking from the victim's perspective depicted the perpetrators as acting with the deliberate
intention to be hurtful, and few, when speaking as perpetrators, disavowed
their responsibility for their actions. Further support for our methods
comes from a series of social psychology experiments (Stillwell & Baumeister, 1997) in which college students were asked to recount *one same*
(hypothetical) event from the victim's or the perpetrator's perspective.

Participants' accounts revealed systematic distortions depending on whose perspective in the event they were asked to assume, and those distortions persisted even when participants were instructed to retell the stories in as accurate a manner as possible, suggesting that differences between accounts given by victims and perpetrators arise even when victims and perpetrators refer to the same event.

Altogether, then, we feel confident in concluding that the unique features of victim and perpetrator narratives—the victims' unilateral focus on their own experience and tendency to overlook the perpetrators' experience, and the perpetrators' incoherent shifting from their own experience to the victims'—may be seen as distortions or biases in the construal of social interactions that are associated with each perspective. It should be stressed that distortions were not associated with only one perspective—it is not, for example, that wicked perpetrators strive to present themselves as innocent but victims have an objective view of conflict situations. Our data speak about the incoherence and shifts in the perpetrator's perspective, as well as about the blindness characteristic of the victim's perspective. Insofar as children's construals from the victim's perspective were so narrowly focused on *their own* experience, it may be argued that victims have a more egocentric perspective than do perpetrators. That argument, we propose, would be a narrow understanding of egocentrism (Wainryb, 1984). The notion of egocentrism captures both the constructive and distortive aspects of the process by which persons come to know and understand reality. In this sense, construals from *both* perspectives can be seen as egocentric, in that construals from *both* perspectives exhibit biases that are related to how reality is experienced from each point of view. Perpetrators were not less (nor more) biased than victims, but rather differently biased. Construals from *both* perspectives featured distortions.

The interpretation that construals from both perspectives exhibit biases associated with the specific ways in which reality is experienced from each viewpoint is supported by findings from attribution research (e.g., Ehrlinger et al., 2005; Pronin et al., 2004; Ross & Ward, 1996). Our findings, however, also suggest that attribution research cannot fully account for construals of situations involving moral conflict. Unlike attribution research, our research focused not only on how children explain their own and another child's behavior, but also on how they explain their own and the other child's behavior as perpetrator and as victim. Whereas attribution research (e.g., Malle & Knobe, 1997; Malle & Pearce, 2001) has indicated that, when explaining their own and another's behaviors, people focus on their own internal mental states but on the other person's observable behavior, we found that this was only true for children's accounts of conflict situations in which they had been the victim. When children gave accounts of situations in which they had been the perpetrator, their explanations of both their own and the other child's behaviors were more complex. In regards to themselves, children referred to their own internal states (largely intentions) but also made references to their actual behaviors. Perhaps more significantly, when speaking about the other child, their focus was not so much on the actual behavior but on the other child's emotions. Our findings, therefore, suggest that, at least when the behavior being explained entails harm or unfairness to others, it may not be sufficient to consider the differences between self and other; the relative perspectives of the self and the other within the conflict situation must be accounted for as well.

Our proposition that victim and perpetrator construals exhibit biases that are related to how reality is experienced from each perspective is also supported by the impressive body of evidence documenting not only the systematic biases characteristic of the ways in which aggressive children construe social situations but also the relations between children's construals and their social interactions (e.g., Coie & Dodge, 1998; Crick & Dodge, 1994; Dodge, 2003). Direct comparisons between the findings of research by Dodge and colleagues and our own cannot be made because research conducted with aggressive children has relied largely on hypothetical situations and has explicitly probed children's thinking about intentions and other elements in their construals. This caveat notwithstanding, it appears that the construals of aggressive children differ from *both* victim and perpetrator construals as assessed in the present study. Aggressive children, who tend to view themselves as victims, emphasize others' hostile intentions toward them; victims in our study focused, rather, on their own feelings and frustration. Aggressive children also tend to depict their actions as being justifiable responses to their peers' hostility; few perpetrators (and only young ones) in our study did so. To fully understand the meaning of these differences it may be necessary to ascertain which elements (e.g., intentions, feelings) are emphasized by aggressive children when speaking about their own interpersonal conflicts and without direct probing. In one important sense, however, our propositions differ from (or perhaps extend) those made by Dodge and colleagues. Whereas Dodge's research is based on the premise that the biases in the construals of aggressive youth (as well as depressed or victimized youth; see Graham & Juvonen, 2001) are associated with individual differences in social information processing, our broader claim is that the construals that children in non-clinical or normative samples make of their social interactions are also not objective records of facts.

Indeed, it is our interpretation that the distortions or biases exhibited by construals made from the victim's and the perpetrator's perspectives (not unlike those characteristic of explanations of self and other, or those of aggressive kids) are systematically associated with each perspective because they are intrinsic to the process of construal—to the ways in which everyone, regardless of age, comes to know reality. We further speculate that the pervasiveness of perspective-related biases may be especially marked and stable in regards to the realm of moral knowledge because, both ontologically and phenomenologically, moral conflicts are made up of competing perspectives. A different interpretation, often taken as self-evident, is that systematic biases and distortions such as those evident in the victim and perpetrator construals are a manifestation of broad motivational and ego-defensive strategies through which people strive to maintain or enhance their self-esteem or positive opinion. This explanation rests on the assumption that, when confronted with threatening predicaments, people proffer self-enhancing explanations that allow them to disengage from blame and responsibility and elicit sympathy and good will (Bandura, 1991, 1998; Baumeister & Catanese, 2001; Baumeister et al., 1990; Schlenker, 1980; Schlenker, Pontari, & Christopher, 2001; Schlenker & Weigold, 1992; Steele, 1988).

Bandura (1991), for example, places motivational concerns at the basis of moral functioning. In his view, people regularly invoke biased construals of reality that serve to depict morally reprehensible behaviors as morally acceptable. Such self-exonerative rationalizations enable the disengagement of internal controls, thereby permitting people to engage in immoral behaviors free from self-censuring restraints. This mechanism "operate[s] in everyday situations in which decent people routinely perform activities having injurious human effects to further their own interests or for profit" (Bandura, 1991, p. 94).

Schlenker and colleagues (Schlenker, 1980; Schlenker & Weigold, 1992) have similarly argued for the view that self-presentational biases and tactics are a ubiquitous feature of social interactions. In fact, Schlenker and Weigold (1992) have explicitly argued against the more restricted view of self-presentational biases as tangential factors to be dealt with through methodological controls. Their more expansive view, that self-presentation is "a fundamental and central interpersonal process" (Schlenker & Weigold, 1992, p. 134), has led to somewhat paradoxical claims, such as that self-presentation is implicated in all types of social behavior (e.g., aggression, criminality, helping behavior, appeals to fairness, schizophrenic symptoms, eating behavior, the reluctance to transmit bad news, and interaction patterns in kindergarten; Schlenker & Weigold, 1992, p. 136), that people use self-presentational strategies not only for their own benefit, but for the benefit of others, including mere acquaintances (Schlenker, Lifka, & Wowra, 2004), and that self-presentation may be manifested not only in self-enhancing strategies but in self-handicapping strategies (Schlenker & Weigold, 1992) and may not only result in face saving and self-enhancement but may also have the opposite consequences (Schlenker et al., 2001).

We neither dispute nor doubt that people, including children, might at times (perhaps even often) wish to present themselves in a positive light, and that this motivation might color their explanations and construals of situations (Wainryb, 2000). Nevertheless, we think that there is a danger in too readily and uncritically accepting motivational factors as the sole, or even the main, explanation for the different construals given by victims and perpetrators. There are two main reasons for urging caution in this regard.

First, self-presentational and motivational biases do not, in and of themselves, predict a particular pattern of construals. This is inevitable especially given the wide-ranging scope that self-presentation is presumed to have. Indeed, even if we were to assume that self-presentational considerations operate on children's construals—that is, even if we assumed that children construe conflict situations in ways that make them look good vis-à-vis both external and internal audiences—it would still be unclear how precisely perpetrators and victims would have to depict their own actions to "look good." Baumeister (Baumeister & Catanese, 2001; Baumeister et al., 1990) has posited that perpetrators save face by minimizing their own responsibility, laying blame on the undesirable traits or behaviors of the victim or on the circumstances, and downplaying the amount of harm done, and victims save face by emphasizing the perpetrator's negative intentions and senseless behavior and exaggerating the enduring nature of the harm inflicted on them (see also Bandura, 1991). This proposition may seem unassailably self-evident (who, after all, does not wish for the blame to lie elsewhere?), but why could not perpetrators save face by acknowledging the harm they caused and assuming responsibility? Why could not victims secure sympathy and good will by asserting to have been injured while at the same time acknowledging that the perpetrators' actions were not evil or meant to cause them harm? Our argument, in other words, is that the same motivation (i.e., to save face) might lead to widely different, even opposite, construals of a situation. Therefore, the conclusion that a particular pattern of construals is the result of motivational biases is unwarranted.

Second, there is considerable evidence for the existence of nonmotivational sources of bias in construals and explanations of reality. Attribution research, in particular, has provided reliable evidence suggesting that self-serving motivational factors need not be introduced to explain most of the fundamental inferential biases. Jones and Nisbett (1987) gave careful consideration to the underlying cognitive, perceptual, and attentional processes which might account for divergent construals of actors and observers (see also Ross & Nisbett, 1991), and more recent research has provided further evidence for such nonmotivational factors underlying the discrepancies between explanations of actors and observers (e.g., Ehrlinger et al., 2005; Malle, 2004; Malle & Knobe, 1997; Malle & Pearce, 2001; Pronin et al., 2004). Furthermore, attribution research has also shown that people's attributions and explanations exhibit biases—the same biases—even when there is no reason to assume that motivational purposes are served by them

(Jones & Nisbett, 1987) and that, in many cases, the same biases in attributions and explanations, far from being self-enhancing, produce unwarranted self-criticism (Ross & Nisbett, 1991; Pronin et al., 2004). Accordingly, even though motivational factors may play a role, it cannot be merely assumed that motivational biases are solely or even largely responsible for the distinct construals of victims and perpetrators.

Together, the possibility that the same self-presentational motives might lead to different types of biases and the evidence of nonmotivational sources of biases suggest that the assumption that victim–perpetrator differences in children's construals are merely a case of self-enhancement or ego-defensiveness is not justified. We furthermore suggest that considering children's victim and perpetrator construals exclusively in terms of rationalizations or presentational tactics blurs the distinction between construals and moral judgments. In turn, this precludes the opportunity to examine the subtle interplay between motivational and nonmotivational factors and the coordinations that children (and adults) engage in when they make moral decisions, thereby limiting our ability to grasp the complexity of the process of moral decision-making.

Even as we urge caution against over-reliance on motivational explanations, the data themselves must be examined for potential consistency with a motivational interpretation. Did perpetrators try to look blameless? For the most part, when speaking from the perspective of perpetrators, children in this study acknowledged their role as perpetrators, acknowledged that they had inflicted harm on another child, and attended to aspects of the victims' plight. Furthermore, perpetrators rarely denied having acted deliberately and, in many cases, admitted acting with the knowledge that their actions would cause pain to another child. Many even acknowledged that their aim was to pursue their own goals and preferences. It is hard to see these features as consistent with wanting to look blameless. However, perpetrators did deny acting with the intent to cause harm. One might argue that in saying that they had acted deliberately but with no intention to cause harm, and in expressing concern for their victims, children—speaking as perpetrators—were trying to minimize their responsibility and look less blameworthy. An alternative interpretation is that, in regards to many of their everyday experiences, children did not merely try to present themselves as blameless, but rather contemplated and struggled with what is essentially a conflict between their own legitimate interests and the demands of morality. Which interpretation one supports might depend on one's conception of the nature of morality and the demands it places on the individual.

One could regard the demands of morality and the interests of the individual as mutually antagonistic, such that morality insists on self-denial, "and if people find it difficult to live up to those demands, that only shows what everyone knows anyway: that people are not, in general, morally very good" (Scheffler, 1992, p. 17). Such a perspective, as Scheffler rightly points out, is rooted in a conception of morality as radically "disengaged from the perspective of the individual agent—from the full range of concerns associated with the living of an actual human life" (p. 18). Scheffler and other contemporary moral philosophers (Hampshire, 1983; Williams, 1985; Wolf, 1982) have suggested, instead, that the discussion of the relations between morality and the interests of the individual requires consideration of the complexity of psychological reality. Importantly, they have underscored that the idea of morality is fully compatible with a realistic picture of human deliberation, including experiences of ambivalence and regret in the face of situations of moral conflict in which there is no act available that is without pain, loss, or harm (Hampshire, 1983; Scheffler, 1992; see also Staub, 2003).

This latter view is more closely aligned with our conception that, starting early on, children develop multiple moral, social, and personal concerns, which get played out (often in conflict) in their social lives. In fact, even as our findings were to some extent consistent with those of early research (Walton, 1985) suggesting that children who have engaged in moral transgressions feel compelled to address their conduct toward the victims and heal the breach between them, the perpetrator construals in our study suggest that this is not the whole story. Personal goals, interests, and preferences were also important to children. Far from attempting to look blameless, the construals that children made about their perpetrator experiences suggest that they are fully engaged in wrestling with a conspicuous feature of moral life—the conflict between the demands of morality and the interests of the individual.

But why is it that, in such situations, the victim's plight and distress impose themselves in some cases but not others? What makes personal goals prevail on some occasions but not others? We cannot, based on our data, explain how or why certain elements in a complex gestalt gain salience and others become overshadowed; we expect that multiple factors—cognitive, emotional, motivational, and contextual—may be involved. We do, nevertheless, suggest that there are two reasons for attending to the interplay of concerns perceived to be implicated in any given social situation, even if those questions remain unanswered. One is that *moral judgments* about real conflict situations are made in regard to the interplay of whatever concerns are perceived to be implicated. Furthermore, we suggest that children's *moral behaviors* are related to their differential attention to (or weighing of) the various concerns (e.g., other people's distress, their own goals and needs) they perceive to bear on their social experiences. In other words, we suggest that the construals and interpretations that children make of their social experiences—the noticing, overlooking, weighing, and prioritizing—constitute the psychological place from which moral action springs.

We propose that understanding children's own construals of the various concerns that are, in their view, implicated in any given situation of moral conflict is an essential step in understanding the relation between children's moral judgments and moral actions. This proposition is consistent with social-cognitive data showing that the behaviors of aggressive children (Crick & Dodge, 1994) and victimized children (Graham & Juvonen, 2001; Ladd & Ladd, 2001) are associated with those children's specific construals of social interactions. It is also consistent with Turiel's (1990, 2003; Turiel & Davidson, 1986; Turiel & Smetana, 1984; see also Nucci, 2004b) analysis that to understand the relation between moral thought and action it is necessary to consider both the moral and non-moral concerns that individuals bring to bear on their construals of situational contexts. Concerns about the relation between the spheres of judgment and action have been long-lasting and persistent within the study of moral psychology but, starting with the classic research conducted by Hartshorne and May (1928–1930), assessments of the consistency between moral judgments and moral behaviors have yielded what can at best be described as small to moderate effects (for comprehensive reviews, see Blasi, 1980, 1993). One approach to these concerns has been to look for motivational constructs, such as strength of character, willpower, moral identity, and self-consistency, that might bridge across the two (e.g., Blasi, 1993; Blasi & Glodis, 1995; Colby & Damon, 1992; Maclean, Walker, & Matsuba, 2004). Whether the data gathered in support of such constructs are compelling or not is a matter of some controversy (for a comprehensive discussion, see Nucci, 2004b). Our framing of these issues is different. We suggest that the relations between children's construals, judgments, and actions in concrete moral situations need to be understood before other constructs are posited to mediate or bridge across them (see also Turiel, 2003).

The research described in this *Monograph* did not include assessments or observations of children's actual behaviors in the conflict situations they described, because we thought it essential to first assess the effects that children's perspectives may have on their construals and moral thinking. Such a task, we thought, would be best accomplished via a within-subject design in which the same child provides one narrative from the victim's perspective and one from the perpetrator's. Nevertheless, we suggest that detailed research involving assessments of children's actual behaviors in conflict situations, along with assessments (such as those included in this *Monograph*) of both their construals and evaluations of those behaviors (rather than evaluations of behaviors depicted in hypothetical stimuli) would be a promising and necessary direction to take in the future in order to shed further light on the relations between moral judgments and moral behavior.

One of the concerns associated with studying moral development in the context of children's own construals of conflict situations has been that doing so may result in a relativistic approach to morality. In some respects, indeed, it may seem as though by asserting that children's moral behavior can be explained in terms of their specific construal of their experiences—that there is "no valid psychological definition of moral behavior from the *outside*" (Turiel, 1990, p. 36)—we advance a moral relativistic viewpoint. If only a child's (or person's) subjective interpretation of an incident is considered, morality becomes a subjective phenomenon: moral behavior is whatever any one child considers, at a particular place and time, to be moral. Is relativism inevitable when matters of interpretation and perspective are incorporated into moral thinking? The argument for why accounting for individuals' construals and interpretations of social reality does not *necessarily* imply moral relativism has been made elsewhere (Asch, 1952; Searle, 1995; Turiel, 2004; Wainryb, 2004). The answer suggested by our findings is twofold.

On the one hand, children did not passively register the facts of their social interactions—they did not report a mere copy of reality. Instead, children construed and interpreted those events—one might even say that children constructed different realities. In this respect, it is the child who construes an experience as moral or nonmoral. On the other hand, children's construals, though subjective, were not arbitrary. The types of actions they described in their narratives (e.g., hitting, calling names, excluding) all belonged in the moral realm and were in keeping with the types of transgressions typically identified by researchers, according to epistemological criteria, as representing moral transgressions. The elements they referred to in the narratives were also of the sort typically seen as the building blocks of moral experience (e.g., intentions, emotions). Finally, the contents and organization of those narratives, though diverse, clustered around two main gestalts. This pattern of findings suggests that even as children actively construct their own understandings of social situations from different perspectives, their construals are neither fictions nor emergent discursive positionings (Bamberg, 1997; Davies & Harré, 1990). Rather, the range of subjectivity and variability in children's construals of reality—though ample—appeared to be bounded and constrained by aspects of reality.

The larger picture emerging from these data is that children's moral lives are played out amid the tensions between reality and interpretation—tensions aptly captured in Asch's notion of relational determination of meanings (Asch, 1952; see also Duncker, 1939). The analyses in this study make it clear that the study of moral development cannot ignore the role of interpretation and perspective in moral thinking. Our data were less clear in regards to whether children themselves are aware of the role of interpretation in their own and others' moral thinking.

81

Although children in this study referred more frequently to desires, wants, and preferences than to construals and interpretations, we do not think that this finding, in and of itself, can be taken to mean that children do not recognize the role of construal and interpretation in their own and the other child's thinking. In everyday discourse, assertions of personal dislikes and goals might be understood as implying beliefs; thus people may find it necessary to speak explicitly about beliefs only when a belief is not made evident through the communication of a dislike or a goal (Bartsch & Wellman, 1989; Wainryb & Brehl, in press). Given the importance of whether children do or do not understand how interpretation affects their own and other people's moral judgments—both in regards to how they think about other people and how they negotiate conflicts and disagreements—these issues should be further explored.

Our data were less ambiguous in regards to *young children's* limited ability to consider psychological information. This is consistent with current research on children's developing theories of mind suggestive of the primitive nature of children's psychological understandings (e.g., Astington et al., 1988; Bartsch & Wellman, 1995; Wellman, 2002). It is also consistent with research showing that when reasoning about hypothetical situations, young children take into account psychological aspects of a situation (e.g., intentions, emotions, goals) when this information is made explicit, but have difficulties doing so when the information is not made explicit (e.g., Bartsch & Wellman, 1989; Brehl & Wainryb, 2005; Karniol, 1978; Keasey, 1977; Nelson Le-Gall, 1985; Shultz et al., 1986). Findings in our study, in turn, suggest that young children also have difficulties doing so when they construe their own social interactions.

These findings do not, in any way, imply that young children are "less moral"; their categorical moral judgments suggest that their moral concerns are firm and unwavering. Rather, the findings point to the more fractured quality of young children's experiences of conflict situations—a quality that may be at the basis of the more primitive and nonpsychological strategies typically used by young children to resolve conflicts (e.g., Shantz & Hartup, 1992; Shantz & Hobart, 1989).

Whether fractured or coherent, the victim and perpetrator narratives of younger and older children alike suggest that experiences involving hurt feelings and injustice are ubiquitous in their lives. The findings also suggest that the realm of experiences in which moral life gets played out is made up largely of not-quite-intentional and not-quite-unintentional harm (at the least, this is the realm within which most children described themselves both as victims and as perpetrators). This is not to say that those experiences are a matter of indifference to the children involved. Even when conflicts were over relatively trivial matters, they seemed to have represented, for children, "moments of true social engagement and involvement" (Shantz,

1993, p.199). Indeed, the richness of children's narratives suggest that those experiences were memorable; our analyses of those narratives also suggest that *what* is memorable differs depending on the specific perspective children had on those experiences.

Because conflicts constitute an important context of social development (Shantz & Hartup, 1992), it bears asking whether children might learn different things from being in the victim's and the perpetrator's roles. Although children themselves, regardless of the perspective from which they spoke, rarely referred in their narratives to any "lessons" they may have learned from their experiences, this finding is not inconsistent with previous research (Shantz, 1993) and should not be taken to mean that children do not learn from their conflicts. Furthermore, whereas the question of how children's thought may affect their behavior has received considerable attention in the research literature, the complementary question of how children's actual experiences and interactions may impact their understandings has remained relatively unexplored. The importance of this bidirectional relation has nevertheless been emphasized by researchers of moral development (Turiel, 1983, 1998, 2002) and social information processing (Crick & Dodge, 1994; Dodge, 2003).

Even though our data do not allow us to speak with certainty about how victim and perpetrator experiences contribute to children's moral development, we speculate that being in the victim's role underscores for children what it feels like to be hurt—a lesson that is likely to feed into the development of moral concerns. The perpetrator's experience presents more of a challenge. Recall, however, that perpetrators and victims in this study were the same children and, unlike what is more typical of aggressive or conduct-disordered children, the construals of perpetrators in this study did not ignore the victims' plight. The large majority of perpetrators also judged that their actions had been, at least in some respects, wrong, and some spoke about their feelings of guilt. Not unlike victims, therefore, perpetrators also learn something about what it means to be hurt. At the same time, by virtue of having access to their own goals, intentions, and mental states, children in the role of perpetrators are likely to also gain some understanding of the complexity of moral conflicts; the perpetrator's experience is likely to make it clear to children that moral conflicts are made up of different claims and points of view.

The introductory chapters in this *Monograph* outlined the need for integrating the notions of interpretation and perspective into the study of children's moral thinking. As implied in children's own narratives, moral life is not about sainthood. Experiences of mistreating or inflicting harm on other people, as well as experiences of being mistreated or hurt, are part of children's *moral* lives. The study of children's construals of those experiences—the systematic analyses of the contents and coherence of their

83

narrative accounts of those experiences—creates a bridge between children's moral development and their actual conflicts, relationships, and social adjustment, and brings us closer to understanding how moral concepts bear on children's real lives.

THE SCORING OF NARRATIVE ELEMENTS:
ANNOTATED EXAMPLE

Below we present an example of the scoring of narrative elements in a specific narrative (the interviewer's probes appear in capital letters). This perpetrator narrative, provided by a fifth grade boy, includes references to seven of the eight narrative elements identified based on previous research in moral development as well as the scoring of pilot data. As can be seen in the detailed scoring of this narrative, several of these narrative elements were present more than once within the narrative. Each instance was recorded, as this procedure allowed us to examine not only the presence of each narrative element (e.g., Do perpetrators refer to intentions when describing their own transgression?), but also the proportional frequency of particular references (e.g., Whereas references to harmful behavior may be present in both victim and perpetrator narratives, is this element more salient in the narratives given from one perspective vs. the other?). Also, when children referred more than once to the same narrative element, their references did not necessarily represent a repetition of the same concept, and thus recording each reference to a narrative element also allowed us to examine the complexity of children's construals of the situation. For instance, in the example given below, in speaking about his own intentions the narrator admits that he acted in part unintentionally (e.g., "I was running with it and I accidentally ..."), but also impulsively (e.g., "I have a bad temper too ..."). Also, in speaking about the resolutions to the conflict, the narrator acknowledges both the negative (e.g., "... we didn't talk much during the time ...") and positive ("... so that's how we became friends again. Now we're best friends") consequences of his actions. Hence, this particular approach to scoring the semantic content of the narratives allowed us to capture much of the richness of children's construals of their own experiences with peer conflict.

85

The fully scored example follows:

So one time, well, me and my friend Christopher, um, we got sort of . . . We have a big, huge rock collection and we had gotten like, I accidentally, I think I accidentally like broke one of his favorite rocks. Like I was running with it and I accidentally dropped it so he got mad. And the next day at school . . . I thought he was mad at me and I sort of, like we didn't talk a lot so it made like, so we weren't, didn't seem like we were friends anymore. And one day I came up to him and just, and just said like, "Why aren't you talking?" and he just said, "I don't know, I thought that you were being a jerk." So I sort of, and I, I have a bad temper too. So I sort of got mad and like started yelling at him and saying, like, stuff. I don't know what I said, it was a long time ago. UH HUH . . . I think, what happened when he felt hurt, um, I think that . . . Because he had just barely been to Montana and that's where he got that rock, in Montana, so he didn't think that he could replace it ever again. But we ended up getting a new one at the museum. So and that's it. IS THERE ANYTHING ELSE YOU REMEMBER ABOUT THAT TIME? We, we just, like we didn't talk much during the time. And one day our class field trip at the museum, we brought some money and I bought him a new rock so that's probably, so that's how we became friends again. Now we're best friends.

SCORING OF NARRATIVE ELEMENTS

Harmful Behavior

". . . broke one of his favorite rocks" (injustice).
". . . dropped it" (injustice).
". . . started yelling at him and saying, like, stuff" (offensive behavior).

Victim's Response

None

Resolution and Consequences

". . . like we didn't talk a lot . . ." (damage to relationship).
". . . one day I came up to him and just, and just said like, 'Why aren't you talking?' " (perpetrator attempts reparation).
"But we ended up getting a new one at the museum" (perpetrator attempts reparation).
". . . we didn't talk much during the time . . ." (damage to relationship).
"I bought him a new rock . . ." (perpetrator attempts reparation).

86

". . . so that's how we became friends again. Now we're best friends" (conflict resolved).

Narrator's Mental States

"I thought he was mad at me . . ." (construal).
". . . it made like, so we weren't, didn't seem like we were friends anymore" (construal).

Other Child's Mental States

". . . he just said, 'I don't know, I thought that you were being a jerk'" (construal).
". . . so he didn't think that he could replace it ever again" (construal).

Narrator's Emotions

"I sort of got mad" (anger).

Other Child's Emotions

" . . . he got mad" (anger).
"I thought he was mad at me . . ." (anger).
". . . he felt hurt . . ." (sadness).

Perpetrator's Intentions

"I accidentally, I think I accidentally . . ." (unintentional).
"I was running with it and I accidentally . . ." (unintentional).
"I have a bad temper too . . ." (impulsive).

THE SCORING OF CONTENTS OF NARRATIVE ELEMENTS: CATEGORIES AND EXAMPLES

In scoring the content of narrative elements, scorers relied not on their own impressions of the situation, but only on the narrators' explicit references to narrative elements. Narratives often included more than one reference to the same narrative element. In some cases, children made repeated references to the same content category (e.g., "He hit me, and he kicked me, and he pulled my hair," or "He called me a baby . . . and then he said I was a baby . . . he kept on calling me a baby"); in other cases, children's references to a specific narrative element involved different content categories (e.g., "She pushed me down and took my ball, and then she called me a really mean name"). In both cases, each reference was scored. It should also be noted that, as in these examples, the same sentence or utterance may have included more than one reference to the same narrative element; the unit of scoring was each instance of a narrative element, not full sentences or other divisions of verbal utterances. What follows are descriptions of the categories used to score the content of each narrative element, along with illustrative examples taken directly from children's victim and perpetrator narratives.

HARMFUL BEHAVIORS

Physical Harm

References to the perpetrator causing bodily harm to the victim, including hitting, slapping, tripping, or pushing (e.g., "He kept on pushing me down," "I tackled him").

Offensive Behavior

References to the perpetrator yelling at, saying harsh words to, or insulting the victim (e.g., "They were kind of putting me down for what I wanted to do," "I called Jamie 'skinny legs'").

Exclusion

References to the perpetrator ignoring or neglecting the victim, including not talking to the victim, refusing to "hang out," or not inviting the victim to a gathering (e.g., "She said, 'we've already decided that we only want us, not you,'" "I just kept on ignoring her").

Trust Violation

References to the perpetrator betraying the victim by lying, breaking a promise, divulging a secret, spreading rumors, or talking behind the victim's back (e.g., "So my other friend told me that he had heard a bunch of guys on the team talking about me. They were saying that, like, I sucked and stuff," "I said I'd do something with Gina that day, but then Katie called and asked me to go to the mall with her, so when Gina called back I wasn't home").

Injustice

References to the perpetrator taking or destroying the victim's property, or refusing to share (e.g., "Dana was crying yesterday just over some keys . . . I took them from her," "We were taking turns with the sled but then Daryl took it and just kept going down and down").

Harmless Behavior

References to the perpetrator's behaviors that, though not intrinsically harmful, were construed by the victim in ways that resulted in hurt feelings (e.g., "Sometimes she thought I was talking about her but I wasn't," "Her mom was having a garage sale, and I asked if could pay for this one thing, and she said that she still wanted it. So I said, 'Well it's out for sale,' and she started to cry because I said that").

Unelaborated

References to harmful behavior which were not sufficiently detailed to allow classification into one of the other categories (e.g., "We got into an argument and his feelings felt hurt," "Someone said they brought a doll and it wasn't show-and-tell and I was upset").

VICTIM'S RESPONSES

Confronted Perpetrator

References to the victim approaching the perpetrator to express his/her own feelings or to challenge the perpetrator's actions (e.g., "So Maddy came up to me and said 'Why did you do that to us?'" "So I went up to him and told him that he really hurt my feelings").

Withdrew

References to the victim running away, leaving, walking out, or otherwise withdrawing from the situation (e.g., "She ran inside crying," "I said, 'I have to go,' and then just hung up").

Asked for Help

References to the victim approaching a third party to intervene or for consolation; typically the third party was an authority figure, such as a teacher or parent (e.g., "He went and told the recess monitor on us," "So I told my big sister about it . . . and so she told the other girl's sister and then her parents got her in trouble").

Retaliated

References to the victim seeking revenge on the perpetrator or participating in harmful acts of a retaliatory nature (e.g., "They ditched me, so I called them and pretended that I'd been attacked to make them feel bad," "I hit a kid and then he tripped me").

Attempted to Reconcile

References to the victim having approached the perpetrator in an attempt to remedy the situation (e.g., "So he called me . . . and asked me to come back to his house and then we played for about an hour," "And the next recess I said to them, 'Why can't we be friends again?' And then we played more").

No Overt Response

Explicit references to the victim not having an overt response (e.g., "He didn't say anything right at that time," "I just sat there").

RESOLUTIONS

Circumstantial Resolution

References to the conflict being interrupted by something external to the conflict itself, such as the school day being over (e.g., "We were fighting and then my dad got home and that was that," "And then the bell rang so we all went inside and that was the end").

Attempted Reparation

References to the perpetrator initiating contact with the victim in an effort to apologize or make reparation (e.g., "She came up to me the next day and said that she was really sorry about what had happened," "We tried to find him so we could tell him he could play").

Conflict Resolved

References to the relationship between the victim and the perpetrator returning to its original state, including instances in which the victim forgave the perpetrator, the victim and the perpetrator reached a compromise, the victim and the perpetrator apologized to one another, and less detailed references to "everything being okay again" (e.g., "And so then everything was fine," "She got over it and now we're friends and everything," "So we decided to play my game first and then watch his show, and then we got along much better").

Damage to Relationship

References indicating that the conflict was not resolved or that it had harmful consequences for the relationship (e.g., "We never talked about it," "He didn't even say he was sorry," "Then we weren't friends anymore").

MENTAL STATES ATTRIBUTED TO THE NARRATOR AND THE OTHER CHILD

The same mental state categories were used to score references to both the mental states of the narrator and of the other child.

Construals

References to beliefs as to what was true about the situation (e.g., "He ended up feeling hurt because he thought I didn't like him, but I thought we were both just joking around," "She thought I didn't want to take him home because he was different, like she thought I was racist or something, but really I just couldn't afford the gas to be driving all over").

Prescriptive Beliefs

References to beliefs about what should have happened (e.g., "She thought I should have said it in a much nicer way," "I felt like maybe I shouldn't have told anyone").

Disbelief

References to astonishment or shock at what had occurred (e.g., "And I thought to myself, 'How could I do that to my former best friend?'" "He turned to me and was like, 'I can't believe you just said that!'")

Uncertainty

Explicit references to being uncertain about what to think, say, or do at the time of the event (e.g., "I didn't understand why he got mad at me," "Like he was walking upstairs bawling and I didn't know why").

Desires and Preferences

References to wants, likes, and dislikes relating to the event (e.g., ". . . but I didn't want to play Legos," "I was going to ask her to the dance because I really liked her").

Realizations

Explicit references to making discoveries, figuring things out, coming to a state of understanding, and other references to the development of thoughts and ideas (e.g., "And then I thought, 'Oh, her dad doesn't live with her,'" "He got the clue that he'd done wrong really fast").

EMOTIONS ATTRIBUTED TO THE NARRATOR AND THE OTHER CHILD

The same emotion categories were used to score references to both the emotions of the narrator and of the other child. Positive emotions were attributed to the self or other very rarely (less than 5%), and thus were not included in analyses.

Sadness

References to sadness or hurt feelings (e.g., "You could tell that he felt really hurt," "Janie said that I wasn't very smart and that made me feel sad").

Guilt

References to feeling guilty, sorry or regretful (e.g., "He looked like he was really sorry," "I felt guilty for being so mean").

Anger

References to feeling angry, mad, furious, jealous, or resentful (e.g., "She was really ticked off," "It made me so mad I just wanted to punch him in the nose").

Unelaborated Negative

References to unspecified or vague negative feelings (e.g., "That made me feel bad," "And I could tell that she wasn't feeling too good about that").

PERPETRATOR'S INTENTIONS

Incidental to Pursuit of Goal or Preference

References to the harm being incidental to the perpetrator's pursuit of personal goals or preferences (e.g., "My friend came over to ask if I wanted to play, and I didn't really wanted to play, so I thought up a lie," "She wanted to play with me all the time but I wanted to make new friends, so I told her no").

Retribution

References to the perpetrator's actions stemming directly from something the victim had previously done or said to provoke the perpetrator (e.g., "All of a sudden they stopped talking to me and things started happening, like they glued my locker shut, so I put this really gross smelling stuff in her locker," "He said I was stupid because I was yelling at him too much").

Mistaken Assumption

References to the perpetrator acting based on mistaken information (e.g., "I thought he was mad at me, so I just stopped talking to him, but it turned out he wasn't mad," "It made me feel kinda sad when she just left and walked home without me, but later I found out that it was just cause she thought it was the day I stayed at the after-school program, cause sometimes I do that").

Impulsive

References to the perpetrator acting recklessly, often out of anger, jealousy, or frustration (e.g., "Well, I started hanging out with Melanie a lot, and my friend Tasha, she was like feeling all jealous I think, 'cause she was saying very harsh words to me and she was saying that me and Mel were like big show-offs and stuff. She was telling everybody that," "I just started just going off and going crazy because it just sounded really like she called me a brat").

Intent to Harm

References to the perpetrator acting deliberately or maliciously with the intent to harm the victim, or acting on the basis of contempt for the victim or lack of concern for the victim's well being (e.g., "There's this girl in my class, and we don't like her that much, so when she asks if she can play with us, we just tell her to go away," "They were calling me fat in front of everybody because they wanted to make fun of me").

Unintentional

References to the perpetrator's actions being accidental or intended to prevent or avoid further harm (e.g., "He accidentally tripped and knocked me down," "I lied to her because I didn't want to hurt her feelings") and references in which the ensuing harm was described as being unexpected or unintentional (e.g. "It was just a really bad joke, I didn't think she'd get that upset").

Incomprehensible

Explicit references to the perpetrator behaving arbitrarily or for unintelligible reasons (e.g., "So she just stopped talking to me and I never understood why," "I don't know why I said that she smells, I don't ever remember her smelling").

Six markers of coherence (Narrative Assessment Profile; Bliss et al., 1998) were rated as inadequate or adequate: topic maintenance, event sequencing, completion, references to place, references to time, and false starts and fluency. The intercorrelations among coherence markers yielded only three moderate correlations (between topic maintenance and event sequencing, and between completion and the contextual markers of place and time). Given that the set of six coherence markers has been shown in previous research to capture distinct dimensions of coherence, and for the purpose of allowing for comparisons with findings from other labs, we retained the original distinction among the six markers.

In the scoring of pilot data we noted that the influence of each marker on the overall coherence of a narrative was not merely additive; inadequacy along some markers (e.g., topic maintenance), or the degree of inadequacy of a particular marker, at times seemed to weigh more heavily in the overall coherence (or lack thereof) of a narrative. Hence, each narrative was also rated in terms of its global coherence.

What follows are examples of adequate and inadequate narratives along each coherence marker, as well as examples of narratives rated globally as coherent or incoherent. To illustrate how coherence and incoherence are manifested at different ages, we contrast examples of adequate and inadequate narratives drawn from children of similar ages.

COHERENCE MARKERS

Topic Maintenance

Example of Narrative With Adequate Topic Maintenance

The following narrative stays on topic and includes no major digressions or irrelevant information.

This wasn't really a bad disagreement, but once my friend like wanted to like paint, because she always likes to paint. And sometimes I'll do it, but I don't really like to because it's not one of my favorite things, and also she has always does it, so, I get bored of it. So, um, once I sort of just like, "No, I don't want to do it," and so um . . . she's like, "Fine, then I'm going home." So we got in a huge disagreement, but I know she could go home because um, her house was just across the street, and I didn't want her to go home, but I really didn't want to paint, so I was like, "What should I do, what should I do?" And so I just said, "Okay, we'll paint, I'm sorry." (First grade girl)

Example of Narrative With Inadequate Topic Maintenance

In the next narrative, it is difficult to identify a main event; various hurtful interactions are described, and irrelevant information abounds.

Well, one time me and Samantha, she's my other friend, and she was um, she and me were in a big fight and, and we almost started to not be friends anymore. And these big kids were involved and they tried to make me feel good. Because she's in second grade and she can hurt feelings more than I can and, we promised that we would be friends, but sometimes I say at sleepovers, "Maybe I should cross her off the list of my friends," because I keep on thinking of all the mean things that she's done to me in my life. And, and I kind of go to her and say, and say, "Do you, do you feel good about," I guess I could say, "Do you feel good about me not being your friend or me being your friend?" Because she has another best friend, her name is Lindsay. But sometimes they can't make up their mind of being best friends, because I want to take over Lindsay's place but, but she, they can't just stay together or stay not together. I guess one time I said, "Are you Samantha's friend? Because I'm not." And then my friend goes to school after we had a sleepover and she tells her and then, and then I guess that hurts her feelings, but I sometimes have to tell her that that hurts my feelings. (First grade girl)

Event Sequencing

Example of Narrative With Adequate Event Sequencing

This narrative follows a chronological sequence, interrupted only by relevant commentary (e.g., ". . . and he said 'Nothing.' I think it's because more of the other guys that he didn't hang out with very much are showing interest because he now has a car and he can drive around").

> Um, my friend can drive and we, we, all us teenage boys like to go ride around with our friends and have fun. And I didn't want to just go cruise around, I asked for a ride to a place that I needed to be for an appointment and he was pretty much the only ride I could get without walking, and I didn't want to walk, so I asked him and he said that was alright. So the next day he, I saw him in the morning and said, "Is the ride still okay?" And he said yeah, and we went through the day and about an hour before the day ended he was going up to one of his classes and I noticed he had his jacket and his keys and all the stuff he usually has when he just takes off from school. And I thought about it and thought, "maybe he's just gonna take off without me." So, I thought about it and stayed there, and tried to find another ride, but I couldn't, so at the end of the day before he could get to his car, I ran down to his car to meet him. And he showed up a little while later with other kids and I asked him, "Can I still have a ride?" and he said, "Oh, no." And I begged and begged and he finally said okay. So, he gave me a ride, but he talked to the other guys more than he usually talks to me, so I was kind of wondering what was going on, so I asked him, and he said, "Nothing." I think it's because more of the other guys that he didn't hang out with very much are showing interest because he now has a car and he can drive around. He has a nice car and everyone wants his car, and everything. He dropped me off and I, before I could say thanks, he kind of took off, so, and I felt kind of bad. (Tenth grade boy)

Example of Narrative With Inadequate Event Sequencing

This narrative jumps back and forth in time; it is unclear in what order the series of events took place. This poor organization makes the narrative as a whole difficult to understand.

> So, one time Kyra, my best friend, she said, "I'm not your friend anymore. I hate you." So that made me sad and so I just told the teacher that I'm sad. And I just cried. And that's it. IS THERE ANYTHING ELSE THAT YOU REMEMBER ABOUT THAT TIME? Well, then Eileen just ignored. So, and I just, I was trying to say I'm sorry to her because I accidentally hit her in the eye, up in the face, and she thought that I kicked her in the eye. But I didn't. I was just closing my eyes and jump-roping and I accidentally hit her. I didn't see her. So then she just ran off. So, I was running after her, I was running pretty fast, and so she just kept running and running until she just stopped. And she took a breath, while I was running and while I was saying

sorry she just ran. I said sorry maybe a hundred times. UH HUH. She said, "I'm not going to be your friend anymore." So I just, that was just outside when, like on the big playground when there was no snow or anything, but when it was trying to get Christmassy. So, I accidentally hit her. It's an accident. And I just kept running and I think she just stopped. And she just, like, forgot about it. And she's back with me again. And that's the end of that story. (First grade girl)

Completion

Example of Narrative With Adequate Completion

The information and detail included in this narrative is sufficient for understanding the main event. Although the narrative lacks information about the perpetrator's intentions, it includes sufficient detail about the perpetrator's behavior as well as references to the narrator's mental states and emotions, and to the victim's response to the perpetrator's behavior and subsequent interactions.

Okay, yesterday I was, we had to give reports in library class, and my friend Amy like, the kids graded our papers after we read it to them, and Amy was like, she said, "That just deserves a B," and she was kind of talking loud so everyone heard it. She was kind of over-doing it and stuff. And after this one girl Tanya did her report, Amy was all, "Oh, that was great. That's an A." And I don't really care if it was better than mine, but she could have said that in her mind or something, 'cause I kind of wanted to get a good grade. But I think I did pretty well actually. IS THERE ANYTHING ELSE YOU REMEMBER ABOUT THAT TIME? Let's see. Well I talked to her about it, and she was kind of mean about it. She didn't really say sorry, and she didn't, like, she hardly listened to me. And she was kind of like, "Well, hers was better than yours." And I mean, I don't want to be perfect or anything, but that kind of hurt my feelings. (Fifth grade girl)

Example of Narrative With Inadequate Completion

The amount of information missing from this narrative makes it difficult to fully understand the main event. Although the narrator attempts to explain her relationship with the victim, the lack of elaboration makes it difficult to understand who was involved in the conflict and in what way. The perpetrators' harmful behavior is also not described in sufficient detail.

Okay, um, my mom's friend, we broke up a long time ago, and she's a teenager now. She came over, and me and my friend Jody were there, and we probably didn't mean to, though, um . . . We're standing outside and she came across the street and then . . . We're kind of barefooted and Jody screamed and said, "Ah!" and ran away. And then I did the same thing, but I don't know why. I thought we were playing a game, but she came in crying and I knew what happened. And so I said sorry to her, but she didn't forgive me until two days later. So, and then Jody left the next day and then she came back and we made up and we were friends again, so. IS THERE ANYTHING ELSE YOU REMEMBER ABOUT THAT TIME? Um, I felt really sorry. (Fifth grade girl)

References to Place

Example of Narrative With Adequate Reference to Place

The following narrative, although inadequate in terms of the other coherence markers, includes a clear and explicit reference to where the incident occurred.

One day at my school someone told me that he hates me. Um, then I told the teacher, and I, uh, didn't get rough with him, I just told the teacher. (Preschool boy)

Example of Narrative With Inadequate Reference to Place

The next narrative, although about the same length as the previous one, does not include a clear indication of where the incident occurred.

Um, Jack hit me. And he also, he also kicked me. (Preschool Boy)

References to Time

Example of Narrative With Adequate Reference to Time

This narrative actually begins with a clear reference to when the offense occurred.

It was today. I was playing with my friend Adam and I said something that really hurt him and he said, "I don't like that." And I stopped. IS THERE ANYTHING ELSE YOU REMEMBER ABOUT THAT TIME? I also pushed him. And I said, "I'm sorry." Because he told me he didn't like it. (First grade boy)

Although the following narrative is adequate in terms of many coherence markers (e.g., topic maintenance, event sequencing, reference to place), there is no indication as to when the incident occurred.

> Well me and Elliot were playing at my house, and he, he chose a game that I didn't want to play, so I kind of got mad. And he, well, and I think his feelings got hurt 'cause I kind of got mad at him and because I didn't really want to play it. IS THERE ANYTHING ELSE YOU REMEMBER ABOUT THAT TIME? Well, he chose a game and, well, we were playing and he said that he wanted to play a different game. And I didn't really want to play a different game, so then he went to where all my games are and chose out a game that I didn't want to play. And I said, I said "No, I don't want to play that," and stuff in a mean way. (First grade boy)

False Starts and Fluency

Example of Narrative With Few False Starts and Adequate Fluency

The following narrative includes no incomplete utterances or stumbling over words.

> I used to live next door to a girl who was a couple years younger than me. And we lived next door to each other for as long as we both can remember, and we became friends. And as we got older and older, I got old enough to baby-sit, and she got a little bit jealous. And one time her parents had me come over and baby-sit her and her sister because they were going to be gone late. And she resented the fact that I was over there. And her sister was being obnoxious as usual and my friend felt I was giving more attention to her sister than to her. So she said, "I'm going to play the piano." "Fine go and play the piano." So I was helping her sister on the computer and I couldn't hear the piano, I heard the TV instead. And I came in and I got really mad that she lied to me, and I started yelling and screaming. For a while we didn't talk. Now we've pretty much fixed things up. (Fifth grade girl)

Example of Narrative With Many False Starts and Inadequate Fluency

While false starts are more apparent in the audio version of the narrative, several incomplete or interrupted utterances (e.g., "I mean I talked to her sometimes, but, um") and many instance of stumbling (e.g., "um") are evident even in the transcript.

100

Okay. Well, um, so like, um, in eighth grade again, um, see, we had a class of like twenty-five people and that was like, you know, our class. And so we were all pretty close, I guess. And, um, except there were some people that just weren't as social as others and like, um, this one girl, Natasha, she didn't, um, really have very many friends. I don't know why . . . I mean I talked to her sometimes, but, um. Let's see, what happened? One day we were out, um, like at recess, on the playground. And I was sitting there talking to Cassie and Fiona again, and they were . . . And um, and like I had my back to where everybody was, and I was like facing the school and then they were in front of me. And we were just sitting there talking and um, I don't even remember what we were talking about. But then like we started to talk about Natasha and oh, what did I say? I was like, I said something about her hair and something about how like how she smells, or something. And then like Laura kind of gives me this look, she's like, and I'm like, what? And she's like . . . And so I turn around and she was standing right there. And, um, you know, I was like "Oops." And so then I, well I felt really bad, because I don't like being mean to people, and like I didn't mean to say it. And then, so yeah, she felt really bad and I was like, "Oh, I'm sorry," and she just didn't really say anything. (Tenth grade girl)

Consistency of Adequacy Among Coherence Markers

It should be noted that narratives may be adequate along some coherence markers but inadequate along others. For example, a narrative may have adequate topic maintenance and include references to place and time but have poor event sequencing and include many false starts. An example of a narrative, which included both coherent and incoherent aspects follows, as illustration:

When we . . . played, and didn't, and um, and I said, um let's play this game and, and then, the, that guy said, I can't remember his, um her name and she said, um, and I just ignored her and I just run off playing. We were playing Indians. And my stick was very cool but the next morning, since I was so mean and God, and he, and God didn't really like it, and then, um, the next morning . . . And I put my stick by the wheel, then, and the next morning it was all gone. IS THERE ANYTHING ELSE YOU REMEMBER ABOUT THAT TIME? Um, I ignored her. Yeah but, um I didn't, um I think it was Chloe. (First Grade Boy)

This narrative was scored as adequate in terms of topic maintenance and event sequencing, as the narrator did manage to avoid digressing from the main event (it is clear that he believed his stick being gone was related to his harmful behavior) and the account followed a logical sequence.

101

However, this narrative was also scored as inadequate in terms of completion, as there was little elaboration of the event, making it somewhat unclear what had happened (e.g., Who was the victim? What did the victim say that the narrator ignored? What exactly made the perpetrator's actions "so mean"?). Also, this narrative was riddled with false starts, or stumbling over what was being said. Finally, references to time and place were absent.

GLOBAL COHERENCE

Examples of Coherent Narratives

The following narratives are generally coherent. The accounts are easy to follow overall, and both are fairly well elaborated.

> A kid came up to me and, um, called me a name, and I didn't like it. And then he pushed me over. Then I got up and then he pushed me over again, 'til the teacher came out. And she gave him time out. And then I got, and he got timeout and he didn't do it, and then he punched me in the eye, and I got a black eye, and then I had to go sit down on the cot. And then my mom came and picked me up and then I went back to school and then he gave me another black eye. Then I had to stay home from school for three days. (First grade boy)

> Me and my friend were talking and one of her friends came up and took her aside for a minute. And then when she came back she told me about it, and it was about one of her friend's problems. And she didn't like that this person was coming up to her and telling her about their problems. And so I went over to Jess and said, "You shouldn't come to Maria with your problems, because she's not a problem solver and you should just leave her alone." And that made her really upset. And she was mad at Maria. (Fifth grade girl)

Examples of Incoherent Narratives

The first of the following two narratives includes many false starts and a great deal of stumbling, dysfluencies, and pauses (indicated by "..."). The second narrative is very impoverished. It is unclear whether the narrator is referring to one event or a series of events, and of what the harmful behavior truly consisted. There is also no mention of other narrative elements, with the exception of the narrator's mental states (e.g., "I realized we should have been nicer to each other").

102

It was when Mike . . . they were being really mean to me one day, Jack too. They made a card, no this, and no, Taylor. And he made . . . and . . . and it was mean. And then I threw it back in their face. And the person that made it was named Jack. Yeah, but actually Mike didn't make it. He was gonna make one and then I saw it and I went over there. They . . . they thought I was being really mean to them when I don't really . . . I don't be mean to them and then they just . . . and they be mean to me. Well . . . well, I'll tell you one thing. I didn't mean . . . Mike's mean to me, when I actually sometimes give him some . . . I accident . . . I sometimes give him some of . . . like we get . . . we can get two cookies and I gave him one of my cookies. So then he had three. And he's being mean to me when I be nice to him. Not . . . and I didn't even feel good. It, it didn't hurt . . . it really hurt my feelings too. And it was really hard, 'cause they kept being mean. Then . . . then Mike gave me his quarters that was mostly for his lunch money and I said, "No. you can have it. 'Cause I don't really need his quarters, 'cause it's his lunch money. That kind of . . . I think that happened in February but I don't really remember any other part. (First grade boy)

I guess freshman year there was a kid. We didn't get along with each other very well. He'd say things to me, and I'd say things to him. But it was just like last year when I realized we should have been nicer to each other. We said some pretty negative things to each other, and so, that's probably it. (Tenth grade boy)

REFERENCES

Arsenio, W. F., Gold, J., & Adams, E. (2006). Children's conceptions and displays of moral emotions. In M. Killen & J. G. Smetana (Eds.), *Handbook of moral development* (pp. 581–610). Mahwah, NJ: Erlbaum.

Arsenio, W. F., & Lover, A. (1999). Children's conceptions of sociomoral affect: Happy victimizers, mixed emotions and other expectancies. In M. Killen & D. Hart (Eds.), *Morality in everyday life: Developmental perspectives* (pp. 87–128). New York: Cambridge University Press.

Asch, S. (1952). *Social psychology.* Englewood Cliffs, NJ: Prentice-Hall.

Asher, S. R., & Wheeler, V. A. (1985). Children's loneliness: A comparison of rejected and neglected peer status. *Journal of Consulting and Clinical Psychology,* **53**, 500–505.

Astington, J. W. (2001). The paradox of intention: Assessing children's metarepresentational understanding. In B. F. Malle & L. J. Moses (Eds.), *Intentions and intentionality: Foundations of social cognition* (pp. 85–103). Cambridge, MA: MIT Press.

Astington, J. W., Harris, P. L., & Olson, D. R. (1988). *Developing theories of mind.* New York: Cambridge University Press.

Astor, R. A. (1994). Children's moral reasoning about family and peer violence: The role of provocation and retribution. *Child Development,* **65**, 1054–1067.

Bamberg, M. (1997). Positioning between structure and performance. *Journal of Narrative and Life History,* **7**, 335–342.

Bamberg, M. (2001). Why young American English-speaking children confuse anger and sadness: A study of grammar in practice. In K. E. Nelson & A. Aksu-Koc (Eds.), *Children's language: Developing narrative and discourse competence* (Vol. 10, pp. 55–72). Mahwah, NJ: Erlbaum.

Bamberg, M. (2004). Form and functions of "slut bashing" in male identity constructions in 15-year-olds. *Human Development,* **47**, 331–353.

Bandura, A. (1991). Social cognitive theory of moral thought and action. In W. M. Kurtines & J. L. Gewirtz (Eds.), *Handbook of moral behavior and development: Theory, research, and applications* (Vol. 1, pp. 45–103). Hillsdale, NJ: Erlbaum.

Bandura, A. (1998). Exercise of agency in personal and social change. In E. Sanavio (Ed.), *Behavior and cognitive therapy today: Essays in honor of Hans J. Eysenck* (pp. 1–29). Oxford, UK: Elsevier.

Bartsch, K., & Wellman, H. M. (1989). Young children's attribution of action to beliefs and desires. *Child Development,* **60**, 946–964.

Bartsch, K., & Wellman, H. M. (1995). *Children talk about the mind.* New York: Oxford University Press.

Baumeister, R. F., & Catanese, K. (2001). Victims and perpetrators provide discrepant accounts: Motivated cognitive distortions about interpersonal transgressions. In J. P. Forgas & K. D. Williams (Eds.), *Social mind: Cognitive and motivational aspects of interpersonal behavior* (pp. 274–293). New York: Cambridge University Press.

Baumeister, R. F., Stillwell, A., & Wotman, S. R. (1990). Victim and perpetrator accounts of interpersonal conflict: Autobiographical narratives about anger. *Journal of Personality and Social Psychology*, **59**, 994–1005.

Beck, A. T. (1967). *Depression: Clinical, experimental, and theoretical aspects*. New York: Hoeber.

Berg, C. A., Meegan, S. P., & Deviney, F. P. (1998). A social-contextual model of coping with everyday problems across the lifespan. *International Journal of Behavioral Development*, **22**, 239–261.

Berndt, T. J., & Berndt, E. G. (1975). Children's use of motives and intentionality in person perception and moral judgment. *Child Development*, **46**, 904–912.

Blasi, G. (1980). Bridging moral cognition and moral action: A critical review of literature. *Psychological Bulletin*, **88**, 1–45.

Blasi, G. (1993). The development of identity: Some implications for moral functioning. In G. Noam & T. Wren (Eds.), *The moral self* (pp. 99–122). Cambridge, MA: MIT Press.

Blasi, G., & Glodis, K. (1995). The development of identity: A critical analysis from the perspective of the self as subject. *Developmental Review*, **15**, 404–433.

Bliss, L. S., McCabe, A., & Miranda, A. E. (1998). Narrative assessment profile: Discourse analysis for school-age children. *Journal of Communication Disorders*, **31**, 347–363.

Brehl, B. A., & Wainryb, C. (2005). *Children's explanations of harmful behavior: Naive realism and interpretation*. Unpublished manuscript, University of Utah.

Bruner, J. (1986). *Actual minds; Possible worlds*. Cambridge, MA: Harvard University Press.

Bruner, J. (1990). *Acts of meaning*. Cambridge, MA: Harvard University Press.

Bruner, J. (2002). *Making stories: Law, literature, life*. New York: Farrar, Straus and Giroux.

Chandler, M. J. (1993). Contextualism and the post-modern condition: Learning from Las Vegas. In S. C. Hayes & L. J. Reno (Eds.), *Varieties of scientific contextualism* (pp. 227–247). Reno, NV: Context Press.

Chandler, M. J. (2001). *Perspective-taking in the aftermath of theory–theory and the collapse of the social role-taking literature*. Invited address to the 15th Advanced Course of the Archives Jean Piaget.

Chandler, M. J., & Helm, D. (1984). Developmental changes in the contribution of shared experience to social role-taking competence. *International Journal of Behavioral Development*, **7**, 145–156.

Chandler, M. J., & Lalonde, C. (1996). Shifting to an interpretive theory of mind: 5- to 7-year-olds' changing conceptions of mental life. In A. J. Sameroff & M. M. Haith (Eds.), *Five to seven year shift: The age of reason and responsibility* (pp. 111–139). Chicago: University of Chicago Press.

Coie, J. D., & Dodge, K. A. (1998). Aggression and antisocial behavior. In W. Damon (Series Ed.), & N. Eisenberg (Vol. Ed.), *Handbook of child psychology: Vol. 3. Social, emotional, and personality development* (pp. 779–862). New York: Wiley.

Colby, A., & Damon, W. (1992). *Some do care: Contemporary lives of moral commitment*. New York: Free Press.

Crick, N. R., & Dodge, K. A. (1994). A review and reformulation of social information processing mechanisms in children's social adjustment. *Psychological Bulletin*, **115**, 74–101.

Crick, N. R., & Ladd, G. W. (1993). Children's perceptions of their peer experiences: Attributions, loneliness, social anxiety, and social avoidance. *Developmental Psychology*, **29**, 244–254.

Dalgleish, T., Taghavi, R., Neshat-Doost, H., Moradi, A., Canterbury, R., & Yule, W. (2003). Patterns of processing bias for emotional information across clinical disorder: A comparison of attention, memory, and prospective cognition in children and adolescents with depression, generalized anxiety and posttraumatic stress disorder. *Journal of Clinical Child and Adolescent Psychology*, **32**, 10–21.

Damon, W. (1977). *The social world of the child*. San Francisco: Jossey-Bass.

Darley, J. M., & Zanna, M. P. (1982). Making moral judgments. *American Scientist*, **70**, 515–521.

Davidson, P., Turiel, E., & Black, A. (1983). The effect of stimulus familiarity on the use of criteria and justifications in children's social reasoning. *British Journal of Developmental Psychology*, **1**, 49–65.

Davies, B., & Harré, R. (1990). Positioning: The discursive production of selves. *Journal for the theory of social behavior*, **20**, 43–63.

Denham, S. A., & Kochanoff, A. (2002). "Why is she crying?" Children's understanding of emotion from preschool to preadolescence. In L. F. Barrett & P. Salovey (Eds.), *The wisdom in feeling: Psychological processes in emotional intelligence* (pp. 239–270). New York: The Guilford Press.

Derryberry, W. P., & Thoma, S. J. (2005). Moral judgment, self-understanding, and moral actions: The role of multiple constructs. *Merrill-Palmer Quarterly*, **51**, 67–92.

Dodge, K. A. (1986). A social information processing model of social competence in children. In M. Perlmutter (Ed.), *The Minnesota symposium on child psychology* (Vol. 18, pp. 77–125). Hillsdale, NJ: Erlbaum.

Dodge, K. A. (2003). Do social information-processing patterns mediate aggressive behavior? In B. B. Lahey & T. E. Moffitt (Eds.), *Causes of conduct disorder and juvenile delinquency* (pp. 254–274). New York: Guilford Press.

Duncker, K. (1939). Ethical relativity? *Mind*, **48**, 39–53.

Dunn, J. (1999). Making sense of the social world: Mindreading, emotion, and relationships. In P. D. Zelazo, J. W. Astington & D. R. Olson (Eds.), *Developing theories of intention: Social understanding and self-control* (pp. 229–242). Mahwah, NJ: Erlbaum.

Dunn, J. (2006). Moral development in early childhood and social interaction in the family. In M. Killen & J. G. Smetana (Eds.), *Handbook of moral development* (pp. 331–350). Mahwah, NJ: Erlbaum.

Dunn, J., Cutting, A. O., & Demetriou, H. (2000). Moral sensibility, understanding others, and children's friendship interactions in the preschool period. *British Journal of Developmental Psychology*, **18**, 159–177.

Dunn, J., & Slomkowski, C. (1992). Conflict and the development of social understanding. In C. Shantz & W. Hartup (Eds.), *Conflict in child and adolescent development* (pp. 70–92). New York: Cambridge University Press.

Ehrlinger, J., Gilovich, T., & Ross, L. (2005). Peering into the bias blind spot: People's assessments of bias in themselves and others. *Personality and Social Psychology Bulletin*, **31**, 680–692.

Eisenberg, N. (1989). The development of prosocial values. In N. Eisenberg & J. Reykowski (Eds.), *Social and moral values: Individual and societal perspectives* (pp. 87–103). Hillsdale, NJ: Erlbaum.

Eisenberg, N., & Mussen, P. H. (1989). *The roots of prosocial behavior*. New York: Cambridge University Press.

Eisenberg-Berg, N., & Neal, C. (1981). Chidren's moral reasoning about self and others: Effects of identity of the story character and cost of helping. *Personality and Social Psychology Bulletin*, **7** (1), 17–23.

Feffer, M. H., & Gourevitch, V. (1960). Cognitive aspects of role-taking in children. *Journal of Personality*, **28**, 383–396.

Fiese, B. H., Sameroff, A. J., Grotevant, H. D., Wamboldt, F. S., Dickstein, S., Fravel, D. L., et al. (1999). The stories that families tell: Narrative coherence, narrative interaction, and relationship beliefs. *Monographs of the Society for Research in Child Development*, **64** (2, Serial No. 257).

Fivush, R., Gray, J. T., & Fromhoff, F. A. (1987). Two-year-olds talk about the past. *Cognitive Development*, **2**, 393–409.

Fivush, R., Haden, C., & Adam, S. (1995). Structure and coherence of preschoolers' personal narratives over time: Implications for childhood amnesia. *Journal of Experimental Child Psychology*, **60**, 32–56.

Flavell, J. H. (1968). *The development of role taking and communication skills in children*. Oxford, UK: Wiley.

Flavell, J. H., Green, F. L., & Flavell, E. R. (1986). Development of knowledge about the appearance-reality distinction. *Monographs of the Society for Research in Child Development*, **51** (1, Serial No. 212).

Gergen, K. J. (1991). Emerging challenges for theory and psychology. *Theory and Psychology*, **1** (1), 13–35.

Gnepp, J., & Klayman, J. (1992). Recognition of uncertainty in emotional inferences: Reasoning about emotionally equivocal situations. *Developmental Psychology*, **28**, 145–158.

Graham, S., & Juvonen, J. (2001). An attributional approach to peer victimization. In J. Juvonen & S. Graham (Eds.), *Peer harassment in school: The plight of the vulnerable and victimized* (pp. 49–72). New York: Guilford Press.

Griffin, D. W., Dunning, D., & Ross, L. (1990). The role of construal processes in overconfident predictions about the self and others. *Journal of Personality and Social Psychology*, **59**, 1128–1139.

Gurucharri, C., & Selman, R. L. (1982). The development of interpersonal understanding during childhood, preadolescence, and adolescence: A longitudinal follow-up study. *Child Development*, **53**, 924–927.

Hampshire, S. (1983). *Morality and conflict*. Cambridge, MA: Harvard University Press.

Harré, R., & van Langenhove, L. (1991). Varieties of positioning. *Journal for the Theory of Social Behavior*, **21**, 393–407.

Harré, R., & Moghaddam, F. (2003). Introduction: The self and others in traditional psychology and in positioning theory. In R. Harré & F. Moghaddam (Eds.), *Self and others: Positioning individuals and groups in personal, political, and cultural contexts* (pp. 1–11). Westport, CT: Praeger.

Harris, P. L. (1989). *Children and emotion*. Oxford, UK: Blackwell.

Harris, P. L. (1991). The work of the imagination. In A. Whiten (Ed.), *Natural theories of mind: Evolution, development and simulation of everyday mindreading* (pp. 283–304). Cambridge, MA: Blackwell.

Harris, P. L., & Nunez, M. (1996). Understanding of permission rules by preschool children. *Child Development*, **67**, 1572–1591.

Harter, S., & Whitesell, N. R. (1989). Developmental changes in children's understanding of single, multiple, and blended emotion concepts. In C. Saarni & P. L. Harris (Eds.), *Children's understanding of emotion* (pp. 81–116). New York: Cambridge University Press.

Hartshorne, H., & May, M. A. (1928–1930). *Studies in the nature of character*. New York: Macmillan.

Hatch, E. (1983). *Culture and morality: The relativity of values in anthropology*. New York: Columbia University Press.

Heider, F. (1958). *Psychology of interpersonal relations*. New York: Wiley.

Helwig, C. C. (2006). Rights, civil liberties, and democracy across cultures. In M. Killen & J. G. Smetana (Eds.), *Handbook of moral development* (pp. 185–210). Mahwah, NJ: Erlbaum.

Helwig, C. C., & Turiel, E. (2002). Children's social and moral reasoning. In P. K. Smith & C. H. Hart (Eds.), *Blackwell handbook of childhood social development* (pp. 476–490). Malden, MA: Blackwell.

Horn, S. S. (2005). Adolescents' peer interactions: Conflict and coordination among personal expression, social norms, and moral reasoning. In L. P. Nucci (Ed.), *Conflict, contradiction, and contrarion elements in moral development and education* (pp. 113–127). Mahwah, NJ: Erlbaum.

Jones, E. F., & Nelson-Le Gall, S. (1995). The influence of personal effort cues on children's judgments of morality and disposition. *Merrill-Palmer Quarterly*, **41**, 53–69.

Jones, E. E., & Nisbett, R. E. (1987). The actor and the observer: Divergent perceptions of the causes of behavior. In E. E. Jones & D. E. Kanhouse (Eds.), *Attribution: Perceiving the causes of behavior* (pp. 79–94). Hillsdale, NJ: Erlbaum.

Kahn, P. H. (2006). Nature and morality. In M. Killen & J. G. Smetana (Eds.), *Handbook of moral development* (pp. 461–482). Mahwah, NJ: Erlbaum.

Kalish, C. W. (2005). Becoming status conscious: Children's appreciation of social reality. *Philosophical Explorations*, **8**, 245–263.

Karniol, R. (1978). Children's use of intention cues in evaluating behavior. *Psychological Bulletin*, **85**, 76–85.

Keasey, C. B. (1977). Children's developing awareness and usage of intentionality and motives. *Nebraska Symposium on Motivation*, **25**, 219–260.

Keller, M., Gummerum, M., Wang, X., & Lindsey, S. (2004). Understanding perspectives and emotions in contract violation: Development of deontic and moral reasoning. *Child Development*, **75**, 614–635.

Killen, M., Lee-Kim, J., McGlothlin, H., & Stangor, C. (2002). How children and adolescents evaluate gender and racial exclusion. *Monographs of the Society for Research in Child Development*, **67** (4, Serial No. 271).

Kohlberg, L. (1969). Stage and sequence: The cognitive developmental approach to socialization. In D. Goslin (Ed.), *Handbook of socialization theory and research* (pp. 347–480). Chicago: Rand McNally.

Kohlberg, L. (1971). From is to ought: How to commit the naturalistic fallacy and get away with it in the study of moral development. In T. Mischel (Ed.), *Cognitive development and epistemology* (pp. 151–235). New York: Academic Press.

Korobov, N., & Bamberg, M. (2004). Development as micro-genetic positioning. *British Journal of Developmental Psychology*, **22**, 521–530.

Krebs, D. L., Denton, K., & Wark, G. (2002). Interpersonal moral conflicts between couples: Effects of type of dilemma, role, and partner's judgments on level of moral reasoning and probability of resolution. *Journal of Adult Development*, **9**, 307–316.

Krebs, D. L., Vermeulen, S. C. A., Carpendale, J. I. M., & Denton, K. (1991). Structural and situational influences on moral judgment: The interaction between stage and dilemma. In W. M. Kurtines & J. L. Gewirtz (Eds.), *Handbook of moral behavior and development: Vol. 2. Research* (pp. 139–169). Hillsdale, NJ: Erlbaum.

Ladd, B. K., & Ladd, G. W. (2001). Variations in peer victimization. In J. Juvonen & S. Graham (Eds.), *Peer harassment in school: The plight of the vulnerable and victimized* (pp. 25–48). New York: Guilford Press.

Lagattuta, K. H. (2005). When you shouldn't do what you want to do: Young children's understanding of desires, rules, and emotions. *Child Development*, **76**, 713–733.

Lagatutta, K. H., & Wellman, H. M. (2001). Thinking about the past: Early knowledge about links between prior experience, thinking, and emotion. *Child Development*, **72**, 82–102.

Lalonde, C. E., & Chandler, M. J. (2002). Children's understanding of interpretation. *New Ideas in Psychology*, **20**, 163–198.

Langer, J. (1994). From acting to understanding: The comparative development of meaning. In W. F. Overton & D. S. Palermo (Eds.), *Nature and ontogenesis of meaning* (pp. 191–213). Hillsdale, NJ: Erlbaum.

Laupa, M. (2000). Similarities and differences in children's reasoning about morality and mathematics. In M. Laupa (Ed.), *New directions for child and adolescent development: Vol. 89. Rights and wrongs: How children and young adults evaluate the world* (pp. 19–31). San Francisco: Jossey-Bass.

Lewis, M. D. (2001). Personal pathways in the development of appraisal: A complex systems/ stage theory perspective. In K. R. Scherer, A. Schorr & T. Johnstone (Eds.), *Appraisal processes in emotion: Theory, methods, research* (pp. 205–220). London: Oxford University Press.

Maclean, A. M., Walker, L. J., & Matsuba, M. K. (2004). Transcendence and the moral self: Identity integration, religion, and moral life. *Journal for the Scientific Study of Religion*, **43**, 429–437.

Malle, B. F. (2004). *How the mind explains behavior: Folk explanations, meaning, and social interaction*. Cambridge, MA: MIT Press.

Malle, B. F., & Knobe, J. (1997). Which behaviors do people explain? A basic actor-observer asymmetry. *Journal of Personality and Social Psychology*, **72**, 288–304.

Malle, B. F., & Pearce, G. E. (2001). Attention to behavioral events during interaction: Two actor-observer gaps and three attempts to close them. *Journal of Personality and Social Psychology*, **81**, 278–294.

McAdams, D. (1996). Narrating the self in adulthood. In J. E. Birren & G. M. Kenyon (Eds.), *Aging and biography: Explorations in adult development* (pp. 131–148). New York: Springer.

McCabe, A., & Peterson, C. (1991). *Developing narrative structure*. Hillsdale, NJ: Erlbaum.

McLean, K. C., Pasupathi, M., & Pals, J. L. (2005). *Selves creating stories creating selves: A process model of narrative self-development in adolescence and adulthood*. Manuscript submitted for publication.

Murphy, B. C., & Eisenberg, N. (2002). An integrative examination of peer conflict: Children's reported goals, emotions, and behaviors. *Social Development*, **11** (4), 534–557.

Neff, K. D., & Helwig, C. C. (2002). A constructivist approach to understanding the development of reasoning about rights and authority within cultural contexts. *Cognitive Development*, **17**, 1429–1450.

Neff, K. D., Turiel, E., & Anshel, D. (2002). Reasoning about interpersonal responsibility when making judgments about scenarios involving close personal relationships. *Psychological Reports*, **90**, 723–742.

Nelson Le-Gall, S. A. (1985). Outcome matching and outcome foreseeability: Effects on attribution of intentionality and moral judgments. *Developmental Psychology*, **21**, 332–337.

Nisbett, R. E. (2005). The ghosts of cultural psychology. In R. M. Sorrentino & D. Cohen (Eds.), *Culture and Social Behavior: The Ontario Symposium* (Vol. 10, pp. 251–258). Mahwah, NJ: Erlbaum.

Nucci, L. P. (2001). *Education in the moral domain*. New York: Cambridge University Press.

Nucci, L. P. (2002). The development of moral reasoning. In U. Goaswami (Ed.), *Blackwell handbook of childhood cognitive development* (pp. 303–325). Malden, MA: Blackwell.

Nucci, L. P. (2004a). Social interactions and the construction of moral and social knowledge. In J. I. M. Carpendale & U. Muller (Eds.), *Social interaction and the development of knowledge* (pp. 195–213). Mahwah, NJ: Erlbaum.

Nucci, L. P. (2004b). The promise and limitations of the moral self construct. In C. Lightfoot, C. Lalonde & M. J. Chandler (Eds.), *Changing conceptions of psychological life* (pp. 49–70). Mahwah, NJ: Erlbaum.

Nucci, L. P., & Herman, S. (1982). Behavioral disordered children's conceptions of moral, conventional, and personal issues. *Journal of Abnormal Child Psychology*, **10**, 411–426.

Nunez, M., & Harris, P. L. (1998). Psychological and deontic concepts: Separate domains or intimate connection? *Mind and Language*, **13**, 153–170.

Overton, W. F. (2004). A relational and embodied perspective on resolving psychology's antimonies. In J. I. M. Carpendale & U. Muller (Eds.), *Social interaction and the development of knowledge* (pp. 19–44). Mahwah, NJ: Erlbaum.

Pennebaker, J. W., & Francis, M. E. (1999). *Linguistic inquiry and word count: LIWC*. Mahwah, NJ: Erlbaum.

Peterson, C., & McCabe, A. (1983). *Developmental psycholinguistics: Three ways of looking at a narrative.* New York: Plenum.

Piaget, J. (1932). *The moral judgment of the child.* New York: Free Press.

Piaget, J. (1952). *The origins of intelligence in children.* New York: International Universities Press.

Piaget, J. (1954). *The construction of reality in the child.* Oxford, UK: Basic Books.

Piaget, J. (1960). *The child's conception of the world.* Oxford, UK: Littlefield Adams.

Piaget, J. (1962/2000). Commentary on Vygotsky's criticisms of "Language and Thought of the Child" and "Judgment and Reasoning in the Child." *New Ideas in Psychology,* **18**, 241–259.

Piaget, J. (1970). Introduction. In M. Laurendau & A. Pinard (Eds.), *The development of the concept of space in the child.* Oxford, UK: International Universities Press.

Piaget, J. (1971). *Psychology and epistemology: Towards a theory of knowledge.* New York: Viking Press.

Piaget, J. (2000). Piaget's theory. In K. Lee (Ed.), *Childhood cognitive development: The essential readings* (pp. 33–47). Malden, MA: Blackwell.

Piaget, J., & Inhelder, B. (1969). *The psychology of the child.* New York: Basic Books.

Polkinghorne, D. (1988). *Narrative knowing and the human sciences.* Albany, NY: State University of New York Press.

Polkinghorne, D. (1996). Transformative narratives: From victimic to agentic life plots. *American Journal of Occupational Therapy,* **50**, 299–305.

Prinstein, M. J., Cheah, C. S., & Guyer, A. E. (2005). Peer victimization, cue interpretation, and internalizing symptoms: Preliminary concurrent and longitudinal findings for children and adolescents. *Journal of Clinical Child and Adolescent Psychology,* **34**, 11–24.

Pronin, E., Gilovich, T., & Ross, L. (2004). Objectivity in the eye of the beholder: Divergent perceptions of bias in self versus others. *Psychological Review,* **111**, 781–799.

Rosenau, P. M. (1992). *Post-modernism and the social sciences: Insights, inroads, and intrusions.* Princeton, NJ: Princeton University Press.

Ross, L. (1990). Recognizing the role of construal processes. In I. Rock (Ed.), *The legacy of Solomon Asch: Essays in cognition and social psychology* (pp. 77–96). Hillsdale, NJ: Erlbaum.

Ross, L., & Nisbett, R. M. (1991). *The person and the situation: Perspectives on social psychology.* Philadelphia: Temple University Press.

Ross, L., & Ward, A. (1996). Naive realism in everyday life: Implications for social conflict and disagreement. In E. S. Reed, E. Turiel & T. Brown (Eds.), *Values and knowledge* (pp. 103–136). Mahwah, NJ: Erlbaum.

Scheffler, S. (1992). *Human morality.* New York: Oxford University Press.

Schlenker, B. R. (1980). *Impression management: The self concept, social identity, and interpersonal relations.* Monterey, CA: Brooks/Cole.

Schlenker, B. R., Lifka, A., & Wowra, S. A. (2004). Helping new acquaintances make the right impression: Balancing image concerns of others and self. *Self and Identity,* **3**, 199–206.

Schlenker, B. R., Pontari, B. A., & Christopher, A. N. (2001). Excuses and character: Personal and social implications of excuses. *Personality and Social Psychology Review,* **5**, 15–32.

Schlenker, B. R., & Weigold, M. F. (1992). Interpersonal processes involving impression regulation and management. *Annual Review of Psychology,* **43**, 133–168.

Schult, C. A. (2002). Children's understanding of the distinction between intentions and desires. *Child Development,* **73**, 1727–1747.

Searle, J. R. (1995). *The construction of social reality.* New York: The Free Press.

Sedlak, A. J. (1979). Developmental differences in understanding plans and evaluating actors. *Child Development,* **50**, 536–560.

Sedlak, A. J., & Walton, M. D. (1982). Sequencing in social repair: A Markov grammar of children's discourse about transgressions. *Developmental Review,* **2**, 305–329.

Selman, R. L. (1980). *The growth of interpersonal understanding*. New York: Academic Press.

Selman, R. L. (1994). The relation of role taking to the development of moral judgment in children. In B. Puka (Ed.), *Fundamental research in moral development* (pp. 87–99). New York: Garland.

Selman, R. L., & Byrne, D. F. (1974). A structural–developmental analysis of levels of role-taking in middle childhood. *Child Development*, **45**, 803–806.

Shantz, C. U. (1987). Conflicts between children. *Child Development*, **58**, 283–305.

Shantz, C. U. (1993). Children's conflicts: Representations and lessons learned. In R. R. Cocking & K. A. Renninger (Eds.), *The development and meaning of psychological distance* (pp. 185–202). Mahwah, NJ: Erlbaum.

Shantz, C. U. & Hartup, W. (Eds.) (1992). *Conflict in child and adolescent development*. New York: Cambridge University Press.

Shantz, C. U., & Hobart, C. (1989). Social conflict and development: Peers and siblings. In T. J. Berndt & G. W. Ladd (Eds.), *Peer relationships in child development* (pp. 71–94). New York: Wiley.

Shaw, L., & Wainryb, C. (1999). The outsider's perspective: Young adults' judgments of social practices of other cultures. *British Journal of Developmental Psychology*, **17**, 451–471.

Shaw, L., & Wainryb, C. (2005). *When victims don't cry: Children's understandings of victimization, compliance, and subversion*. Manuscript submitted for publication.

Shultz, T. R., Wright, K., & Schleifer, M. (1986). Assignment of moral responsibility and punishment. *Child Development*, **57**, 177–184.

Shweder, R. A. (1999). Culture and development in our postcultural age. In A. S. Masten (Ed.), *Cultural processes in child development* (pp. 137–148). Erlbaum: Mahwah, NJ.

Siegel, M., & Peterson, C. C. (1998). Preschoolers' understanding of lies and innocent and negligent mistakes. *Developmental Psychology*, **34**, 332–341.

Slaby, R. G., & Guerra, N. G. (1988). Cognitive mediators of aggression in adolescent offenders: I. Assessment. *Developmental Psychology*, **24**, 580–588.

Smetana, J. G. (1997). Parenting and the development of social knowledge reconceptualized: A social domain analysis. In J. E. Grusec & L. Kuczynski (Eds.), *Parenting and the internalization of values* (pp. 162–192). New York: Wiley.

Smetana, J. G. (1999). Context, conflict, and constraint in adolescent-parent authority relationships. In M. Killen & D. Hart (Eds.), *Morality in everyday life: Developmental perspectives* (pp. 225–255). New York: Cambridge University Press.

Smetana, J. G. (2006). Social domain theory: Consistencies and variations in children's moral and social judgments. In M. Killen & J. G. Smetana (Eds.), *Handbook of moral development* (pp. 119–154). Mahwah, NJ: Erlbaum.

Smetana, J. G., Kelly, M., & Twentyman, C. T. (1984). Abused, neglected, and nonmaltreated children's conceptions of moral and conventional transgressions. *Child Development*, **55**, 277–287.

Smetana, J. G., Killen, M., & Turiel, E. (1991). Children's reasoning about interpersonal and moral conflicts. *Child Development*, **62**, 629–644.

Smetana, J. G., Schlagman, N., & Adams, P. W. (1993). Preschool children's judgments about hypothetical and actual transgressions. *Child Development*, **64**, 202–214.

Smetana, J. G., Toth, S., Cicchetti, D., Bruce, J., Kane, P., & Daddis, C. (1999). Maltreated and nonmaltreated preschoolers' conceptions of hypothetical and actual moral transgressions. *Developmental Psychology*, **35**, 269–281.

Staub, E. (2003). *The psychology of good and evil: Why children, adults, and groups help and harm others*. New York: Cambridge University Press.

Steele, C. M. (1988). The psychology of self-affirmation: Sustaining the integrity of the self. In L. Berkowitz (Ed.), *Advances in experimental social psychology: Vol 21. Social psychological studies of the self: Perspectives and programs* (pp. 261–302). San Diego, CA: Academic Press.

Stein, N. L., & Albro, E. R. (1997). Building complexity and coherence: Children's use of goal-structured knowledge in telling stories. In M. Bamberg (Ed.), *Narrative development: Six approaches* (pp. 5–44). Mahwah, NJ: Erlbaum.

Steinberg, M. D., & Dodge, K. A. (1983). Attributional bias in aggressive adolescent boys and girls. *Journal of Social and Clinical Psychology*, **1**, 312–321.

Stillwell, A. M., & Baumeister, R. F. (1997). The construction of victim and perpetrator memories: Accuracy and distortion in role-based accounts. *Personality and Social Psychology Bulletin*, **23**, 1157–1172.

Strong, C. J. (1998). *The Strong narrative assessment procedure (SNAP)*. Eau Claire, WI: Thinking Publications.

Tisak, M. (1995). Domains of social reasoning and beyond. In R. Vasta (Ed.), *Annals of child development* (Vol. 11, pp. 95–130). London: Jessica Kingsley.

Tisak, M., Tisak, J., & Goldstein, S. (2006). Aggression, delinquency, and morality: A social-cognitive perspective. In M. Killen & J. G. Smetana (Eds.), *Handbook of moral development* (pp. 611–632). Mahwah, NJ: Erlbaum.

Toth, S. L., Cicchetti, D., Macfie, J., Rogosch, F. A., & Maughan, A. (2000). Narrative representations of moral-affiliative and conflictual themes and behavioral problems in maltreated preschoolers. *Journal of Clinical and Child Psychiatry*, **29**, 307–318.

Turiel, E. (1983). *The development of social knowledge: Morality and convention*. Cambridge: Cambridge University Press.

Turiel, E. (1990). Moral judgment, action, and development. In D. Schrader (Ed.), *New directions for child development: Vol. 47. The legacy of Lawrence Kohlberg* (pp. 31–49). San Francisco: Jossey-Bass.

Turiel, E. (1998). The development of morality. In W. Damon (Series Ed.) & N. Eisenberg (Vol. Ed.), *Handbook of child psychology: Vol. 3. Social, emotional, and personality development* (5th ed., pp. 863–932). New York: Wiley.

Turiel, E. (2002). *The culture of morality: Social development, context, and conflict*. Cambridge, UK: Cambridge University Press.

Turiel, E. (2003). Morals, motives, and actions. In L. Smith, C. Rogers & P. Tomlinson (Eds.), *Development and motivation* (pp. 29–40). Leicester, UK: British Psychological Society.

Turiel, E. (2005). Thought about actions: Morality, social conventions, and social interactions. Manuscript submitted for publication.

Turiel, E., & Davidson, P. (1986). Heterogeneity, inconsistency, and asynchrony in the development of cognitive structures. In I. Levin (Ed.), *Stage and structure: Reopening the debate* (pp. 106–143). Norwood, NJ: Ablex.

Turiel, E., Hildebrandt, C., & Wainryb, C. (1991). Judging social issues: Difficulties, inconsistencies, and consistencies. *Monographs of the Society for Research in Child Development*, **56** (2, Serial No. 224).

Turiel, E., Killen, M., & Helwig, C. (1987). Morality: Its structure, functions, and vagaries. In J. Kagan & S. Lamb (Eds.). *The emergence of morality in young children* (pp. 155–243). Chicago: University of Chicago Press.

Turiel, E., & Smetana, J. G. (1984). Social knowledge and action: The coordination of domains. In W. M. Kurtines & J. L. Gewirtz (Eds.), *Morality, moral behavior, and moral development* (pp. 261–282). New York: Wiley.

Turiel, E., & Wainryb, C. (1994). Social reasoning and the varieties of social experience in cultural contexts. In H. W. Reese (Ed.), *Advances in child development and behavior* (Vol. 25, pp. 289–326). New York: Academic Press.

Turiel, E., & Wainryb, C. (2000). Social life in cultures: Judgments, conflict, and subversion. *Child Development*, **71**, 250–256.

Wainryb, C. (1984). *Egocentrism revisited*. Unpublished manuscript. University of California, Berkeley.

Wainryb, C. (1991). Understanding differences in moral judgments: The role of informational assumptions. *Child Development*, **62**, 840–851.

Wainryb, C. (1993). The application of moral judgments to other cultures: Relativism and universality. *Child Development*, **64**, 924–933.

Wainryb, C. (2000). Values and truths: The making and judging of moral decisions. In M. Laupa (Ed.), *New directions for child development: Vol. 89. Rights and wrongs: How children evaluate the world* (pp. 33–46). San Francisco: Jossey-Bass.

Wainryb, C. (2004). Is and ought: Moral judgments about the world as understood. In J. Baird & B. Sokol (Eds.), *New directions for child and adolescent development: Vol. 103. Mind, morals, and action: The interface between children's theories of mind and socio-moral development* (pp. 3–17). San Francisco: Jossey-Bass.

Wainryb, C., & Brehl, B. A. (in press). "I thought she knew that would hurt my feelings": Developing psychological knowledge and moral thinking. In R. Kail (Ed.), *Advances in child development and behavior* (Vol. 34). New York: Academic Press.

Wainryb, C., & Ford, S. (1998). Young children's evaluations of acts based on beliefs different from their own. *Merrill-Palmer Quarterly*, **44**, 484–503.

Wainryb, C., Shaw, L. A., Laupa, M., & Smith, K. R. (2001). Children's, adolescents', and young adults' thinking about different types of disagreements. *Developmental Psychology*, **37**, 373–386.

Wainryb, C., Shaw, L., & Maianu, C. (1998). Tolerance and intolerance: Children and adolescents' judgments of dissenting beliefs, speech, persons, and conduct. *Child Development*, **69**, 1541–1555.

Wainryb, C., & Turiel, E. (1994). Dominance, subordination, and concepts of personal entitlements in cultural contexts. *Child Development*, **65**, 1701–1722.

Walker, L. J. (2004). Progress and prospects in the psychology of moral development. *Merrill-Palmer Quarterly*, **50**, 546–557.

Walker, L. J., & Pitts, R. C. (1998). Naturalistic conceptions of moral maturity. *Developmental Psychology*, **34**, 403–419.

Walker, L. J., Pitts, R. C., Hennig, K. H., & Matsuba, M. K. (1999). Reasoning about morality and real-life problems. In M. Killen & D. Hart (Eds.), *Morality in everyday life: Developmental perspectives* (pp. 371–407). New York: Cambridge University Press.

Walker, L. J., de Vries, B., & Trevethan, S. D. (1987). Moral stages and moral orientations in real-life and hypothetical dilemmas. *Child Development*, **58**, 842–858.

Walton, M. D. (1985). Negotiation of responsibility: Judgments of blameworthiness in a natural setting. *Developmental Psychology*, **21**, 725–736.

Wark, G. R., & Krebs, D. L. (1996). Gender and dilemma differences in real-life moral judgment. *Developmental Psychology*, **32** (2), 220–230.

Weiner, B., & Graham, S. (1985). An attributional approach to emotional development. In C. E. Izard, J. Kagan & B. Zajonc (Eds.), *Emotions, cognitions, and behavior* (pp. 167–191). New York: Cambridge University Press.

Wellman, H. M. (2002). Understanding the psychological world: Developing a theory of mind. In U. Goswami (Ed.), *Blackwell handbook of childhood cognitive development* (pp. 167–187). Malden, MA: Blackwell.

Williams, B. (1985). *Ethics and the limits of philosophy*. Cambridge, MA: Harvard University Press.

Wolf, S. (1982). Moral saints. *Journal of Philosophy*, **79**, 419–439.

ACKNOWLEDGMENTS

We thank the principals, teachers, parents, and students of Expanding Horizons Preschool, Child and Family Development Center, Lourdes Elementary School, and Judge Memorial High School for their participation. We also thank Marcie Langley and Susan Canabe for their assistance with data collection, and Jessica Gale for her contribution to the development of the scoring system.

Correspondence concerning this Monograph should be addressed to Cecilia Wainryb, Department of Psychology, University of Utah, 380 South 1530 East, Room 502, Salt Lake City, UT 84112. E-mail: wainryb@psych.utah.edu

COMMENTARY

HUMAN AGENCY AND THE "JOINTS" OF SOCIAL EXPERIENCE: A COMMENTARY ON WAINRYB, BREHL, AND MATWIN

Bryan W. Sokol and Stuart Hammond

This *Monograph* describes the latest in a highly innovative program of research begun by the first author, Cecilia Wainryb, exploring the role that subjective interpretations of reality, or what she and her colleagues call "informational assumptions," have in young persons' moral reasoning and behavior (Wainryb, 1991, 1993; Wainryb & Turiel, 1993). As Wainryb and her co-authors, Beverly Brehl and Sonia Matwin, describe here, such research at the intersection of children's epistemic and moral lives is part of a broader enterprise in psychology originating in the work of Piaget (1932) and Kohlberg (1958, 1969). Within this broader tradition, two questions have always been central: (a) What distinguishes morality from mere social convention, and (b) how do necessary moral truths emerge from the contingent nature of social relations? These questions, as Wainryb and her co-authors suggest, follow from a concern within the constructivist tradition to eschew moral relativism, while nevertheless asserting the autonomy and active interpretive practices of individuals who construct the "moral domain" through their day-to-day social exchanges. Needless to say, accomplishing this feat without falling victim to relativism is a tricky business. Kohlberg (1971) finessed the problem of moral relativism in his classic "is to ought" argument by bracketing off moral or evaluative concepts from day-to-day matters of "fact." Wainryb et al. continue on a similar tack in the present *Monograph*, but with an important exception. They do not, as Kohlberg is often accused of doing (e.g., Krebs, Vermeulen, Carpendale, & Denton, 1991), neglect the social (or day-to-day) dimension of the constructivist enterprise. Indeed, one of the main virtues of Wainryb et al.'s analysis of victims' and perpetrators' conceptions of harm is that it moves this social or interpersonal dimension back to the fore. Still further is the fact that they accomplish this by adopting a narrative approach that pushes the limits of more standard cognitive-developmental methods (i.e., those that involve asking children to reason about tailor-made hypothetical dilemmas). Our goal in this commentary is to continue with some of this pushing by attempting to frame parts of Wainryb et al.'s account within an action-theory perspective (for reviews and further discussion see: Boesch, 1991; Oppenheimer, 1991; Overton, 1998; Sokol & Chandler, 2004, pp. 166–170). Specifically, we will elaborate on the relative stability of certain positions (e.g., victims and victimizers) within social interactions—or what might be understood as the natural "joints" of interpersonal experience—and the role of human agency in the interpretation of these positions. Building on Wainryb et al.'s discussion of the relation between perspective and construal, we will work to show how human agency is constrained at both a psychological—or intra-personal—level and a social—or inter-personal—level, and how reflexive processes within each of these levels could be seen to promote developmental changes.

NARRATIVITY AND CONSTRUCTIVISM: BRINGING ORDER TO EXPERIENCE

In the current era of post-Kohlbergian research, the domains approach—to which Wainryb et al. are important contributors—offers a well-articulated, theory-driven model for exploring children's social and moral reasoning. As is by now well-known, this approach demonstrates how social experience may be organized according to three distinct conceptual domains: the moral, social-conventional, and the personal (Turiel & Davidson, 1986; Turiel, Hildebrant, & Wainryb, 1991). Although sometimes criticized for having defined morality too narrowly in this conceptual scheme (e.g., Campbell & Christopher, 1996), one of the merits of the domains model is that it allows for a highly contextualized account of moral decision making (Nucci, 2004). As Helwig, Turiel, and Nucci (1996) have remarked, by "narrowing the conception of morality" the domains approach actually stands "to broaden explanations of social and personal development" (p. 89). The present *Monograph* provides a clear instance of how domains researchers are working to make good on this promise. That is, Wainryb et al.'s efforts here continue the practice within the domains approach to broaden its explanatory scope. In the present case, Wainryb and her co-authors accomplish this task by introducing two more critical features of the moral context: (a) the role of individuals' interpretive processes in making sense of (or, in this case, "narrativizing") morally relevant situations, and (b) the constraints that social positions, such as being a victim or a perpetrator of harm, place on individuals' reasoning and understanding of such situations. As Wainryb et al. describe, these two parts of the moral context constitute an individual's construal and perspective, respectively, and can be shown (as Wainryb et al.'s results make clear) to interact in predictable ways throughout childhood and adolescence.

Although it may seem presumptuous to imagine that Wainryb et al.'s account needs any further elaboration or support, we cannot help but see in their work a rich intellectual backdrop for advancing some of our own thoughts about human agency. One of these thoughts concerns the expression of human agency in the interpretive acts, or construals, that individuals deploy in making personal sense of the world around them. Consistent with much of Wainryb et al.'s constructivist leanings, we, too, want to argue that human existence is interpretive all the way down, or to borrow from Charles Taylor (1985), that human beings are fundamentally "self-interpreting animals" (p. 45). Such a position on the thoroughgoing nature of construal, we note, is what leads Wainryb et al. to distinguish their work from Dodge's account (Crick & Dodge, 1994; Dodge, 2003) of attribution biases that result from faulty or deficient social information processing mechanisms in atypically developing youth. The critical point that Wainryb et al. make regarding this matter is that the process of construal or interpretation is not itself suggestive of fault—both typical and atypical children engage in interpretive practices, neither of which yield entirely "objective" renderings of reality. Herein, however, lies the rub. What steers this commitment to interpretationism away from utter solipsism? That is, how does a constructivist account of epistemic life, just like a constructivist approach to morality, avoid the charge of relativism? Interestingly, Wainryb herself has been called to respond to this issue in other contexts (see Wainryb, 2000), playing, it seems, to mixed reviews (Kahn, 2000, pp. 80–81).

To be clear, our goal here is not to continue pressing Wainryb or her colleagues on this contentious matter, only to illustrate how a common challenge to constructivism is reflected in her work. If we were to press ourselves, however, we would offer a response with the following two parts. First, it is important to recognize that relativism, and whatever anxiety (Cartesian or otherwise) it might produce in an objectivist's quest for infallible knowledge, is a function of a dualistic separation of mind and world. "The fear of solipsism," as Overton (1994) has remarked, "rather than being the effect of interpretationism, is a direct consequence of the tradition of objectivism itself" (p. 218; see also Bernstein, 1983). Constructivism, in contrast to the objectivist tradition, begins from the epistemic starting point that reality "cannot be known independently of the activity of the knowing subject" (Carpendale, 1997, p. 39). "True" or "objective" knowledge, then, cannot be based on the accuracy of one's mental representations, or on their ability to match some mind-independent piece of reality. Rather, objectivity (if it can be called this) must be found in the coherence of one's mental life and the functionality of human intelligence across diverse interactive contexts. In this regard, Wainryb et al.'s choice to align the domains approach with narrative or discourse psychology in the present *Monograph* seems particularly appropriate. That is, narratives, as McAdams (1997, 1998) has argued, are the ideal form for capturing both the inherent interpretive activities of individuals and the universal impulse to give experience coherent meaning. To draw from Sartre: "the essential form of the self is that of a retrospective story that creates order out of the chaos of experience" (cited in Charme, 1984, p. 2). Narrativity, then, can be seen to offer both creativity and constraint, or in the language of Piaget, assimilation and accommodation—the central psychological processes within a constructivist account (Carpendale, 1997).

Second, and following closely from our reasoning that narrative structure provides a viable mechanism for constraining (and ordering) human agency, is the fact that interpretive acts—even if understood to be thoroughgoing—are not without critical moments of stability. Construals, as Wainryb et al. describe, always occur from a perspective. In the present case, the perspectives under consideration are the relatively stable positions represented in prototypical conflict situations: victim and perpetrator. In other work, Wainryb and her colleagues (e.g., Wainryb & Turiel, 1994) have explored perspectives from a broader societal or cultural standpoint involving power differentials between the traditional positions of men and women in Middle Eastern societies. Although Wainryb et al. do not take the steps to further organize these different levels of perspective, they could be arranged hierarchically to reflect the degree in which social influences impact one over the other (for further discussion of such levels see Wiley, 1994). That is, insofar as victim–perpetrator perspectives map onto more primitive or basic causal categories like "patient" and "agent," it could be argued that some perspectival positions resist de-stabilizing social forces more than others, or at least that they draw their stability from more or less "reliable" sources (e.g., natural positions in a dialogue vs. socially constructed roles in society).

Although exploring the utility of such a hierarchical arrangement is perhaps a future direction for Wainryb et al.'s work to take, the real point we want to make here is that, no matter what the arrangement, these perspectives—or positions of interpretive stability as we would call them—are all somehow "external" or inter-personal in nature. Interpretive acts, however, might also be constrained by more intra-personal mechanisms. One of the clearer discussions of such "internal" constraints on human agency can be found in Shusterman's (1994) rendition of the hermeneutic circle. According to Shusterman, "uninterpreted understandings and experiences . . . provide a ground to base and guide our interpretations and to distinguish between different levels or sequential acts of interpretation" (p. 257). In other words, human agency on this intra-personal plane moves between moments of understanding, which are relatively stable and guide interpretive acts, to moments of interpretation, which generate flux and lead to the revision of prior understanding. Taken together, understanding and interpretation constitute the stabilizing and de-stabilizing features of an ongoing dialectical cycle.

REFLEXIVITY AND DEVELOPMENT: EVOLVING SOCIAL CATEGORIES

So far in our reaction to this *Monograph*, there has been little in which to find fault. This is largely because Wainryb et al. themselves argue from such stable conceptual and empirical grounds their work is hard not to find convincing. Still, at least part of our assignment here, is to assume a critical stance toward their work. On this note, the one criticism we must voice is that Wainryb et al. do not go far enough in their exploration of the available perspectives, or positions, that can be found within hurtful situations. Victims and perpetrators, while perhaps the most salient dimensions in morally hazardous situations, are just two perspectives from which to interpret moral conflicts. Some of the more recent work in the bullying literature, however, offers other perspectives to consider (e.g., Salmivalli, Lagerspetz, Bjüorkqvist, Österman, & Kaukiainen, 1996; Sutton & Smith, 1999; Salmivalli, 1999). Specifically, bullying situations have been shown to involve a complex structure, including—not only victims and victimizers—but also assistants, reinforcers, observers, and defenders, to name just a few.

Militating for such an expansion of relevant social roles in conflict situations, however, is only a small part of the issue we want to raise here. Our bigger concern is that Wainryb et al. seem to overlook the possibility that positions or perspectives in a situation, despite serving a stabilizing function, can themselves be re-interpreted, or re-storied, when acts of construal become reflexive, or directed back on the individual agent. A possible reason for why Wainryb et al. found few developmental differences in participants' descriptions of victim and perpetrator perspectives may be because their methods do not easily allow for this reflexive capacity to be observed. Given Wainryb et al.'s narrative commitments, however, the absence of any account of "reflexive agency"—either in their otherwise rich theoretical discussion or their empirical findings—is perplexing. Narrative theorists from a variety of backgrounds have all frequently acknowledged the role of reflexivity in human experience. Amélie Rorty (1976), for instance, has described human beings "as just the sort of organisms that interpret and modify their agency through their conceptions of themselves" (p. 323). Charles Taylor (1985, p. 69) has argued even further that reflexivity is what allows victimized individuals to find empowerment in their status, or to reverse their positions as "patients" in the social matrix. More specifically, he describes how such revolutions in self-interpretation are what lead to

119

expressions like "black is beautiful" and "gay pride." Finally, and manifesting a less positive side of reflexivity, Baumeister, Stillwell, and Wotman (1990) have observed that even perpetrators may re-story their positions to "embrace the victim's role" (p. 1003). In an example they provide, many post-Civil War slave owners tried to recharacterize themselves as "martyrs for a noble way of life and victims of ungrateful treatment (e.g., desertion)" (p. 1003). Of course, such renarrations, or reflexive changes in one's perspective, are likely to be relatively late developmental occurrences, perhaps even beyond the age groups that Wainryb et al. studied. Nevertheless, some attention to the study of reflexive agency would enrich Wainryb et al.'s future work and likely strengthen their developmental posturing—or "robust view" as they say—toward narrative research.

Because ending on a critical note is hardly befitting of such admirable work, let us offer one final thought. In a field that has become increasingly fragmented since Kohlberg's untimely passing, Wainryb et al. have taken several important steps in the present *Monograph* to integrate two extremely rich approaches in the study of children's moral development. By offering a bridge between cognitive-developmental and narrative accounts of morality, this *Monograph* has the potential to unify some of the more diverse ideas in the field, and perhaps even stabilize what is quickly becoming a literature on the verge of solipsistic collapse.

References

Baumeister, R. F., Stillwell, A., & Wotman, S. R. (1990). Victim and perpetrator accounts of interpersonal conflict: Autobiographical narratives about anger. *Journal of Personality and Social Psychology,* **59**, 994–1005.

Bernstein, R. J. (1983). *Beyond objectivism and relativism: Science, hermeneutics, and praxis.* Philadelphia: University of Pennsylvania Press.

Boesch, E. E. (1991). *Symbolic action theory and cultural psychology.* Berlin, Germany: Springer-Verlag.

Campbell, R. L., & Christopher, J. C. (1996). Moral development theory: A critique of its Kantian presuppositions. *Developmental Review, 16,* 1–47.

Carpendale, J. (1997). An explanation of Piaget's constructivism: Implications for social cognitive development. In S. Hala (Ed.), *The development of social cognition* (pp. 35–64). Hove, UK: Psychology Press.

Charme, S. L. (1984). *Meaning and myth in the study of lives: A Sartrean perspective.* Philadelphia: University of Pennsylvania Press.

Crick, N. R., & Dodge, K. A. (1994). A review and reformulation of social information processing mechanisms in children's social adjustment. *Psychological Bulletin,* **115**, 74–101.

Dodge, K. A. (2003). Do social information-processing patterns mediate aggressive behavior? In B. B. Lahey & T. E. Moffitt (Eds.), *Causes of conduct disorder and juvenile delinquency* (pp. 254–274). New York: Guilford Press.

Helwig, C. C., Turiel, E., & Nucci, L. P. (1996). The virtues and vices of moral development theorists. *Developmental Review, 16,* 69–107.

Kahn, P. H. (2000). Mind and morality. In J. A. Baird & B. W. Sokol (Eds.), *New directions for child and adolescent development, No. 103: Connections between theory of mind and sociomoral development* (pp. 73–83). San Francisco: Jossey-Bass Inc.

Kohlberg, L. (1958). *The development of modes of moral thinking and choice in the years ten to sixteen.* Unpublished doctoral dissertation, University of Chicago.

Kohlberg, L. (1969). Stage and sequence: The cognitive developmental approach to socialization. In D. Goslin (Ed.), *Handbook of socialization theory and research* (pp. 347–480). Chicago: Rand McNally.

Kohlberg, L. (1971). From is to ought: How to commit the naturalistic fallacy and get away with it in the study of moral development. In T. Mischel (Ed.), *Cognitive development and epistemology* (pp. 151–235). New York: Academic Press.

Krebs, D. L., Vermeulen, S. C. A., Carpendale, J. I., & Denton, K. (1991). Structural and situational influences on moral judgment: The interaction between stage and dilemma. In W. M. Kurtines & J. L. Gerwirtz (Eds.), *Handbook of moral behavior and development, Volume 2: Research* (pp. 139–169). Hillsdale, NJ: Lawrence Erlbaum.

McAdams, D. P. (1997). The case for unity in the (post) modern self: A modest proposal. In R. D. Ashmore & L. Jussin (Eds.), *Self and identity: Fundamental issues* (pp. 46–78). New York: Oxford University Press.

McAdams, D. P. (1998). Ego, trait and identity. In P. M. Westenberg, A. Blasi & L. D. Cohn (Eds.), *Personality development: Theoretical, empirical, and clinical investigations of Loevinger's conception of ego development* (pp. 27–38). Mahwah: Lawrence Erlbaum Associates.

Nucci, L. (2004). Reflections on the moral self construct. In D. K. Lapsley & D. Narvaez (Eds.), *Moral development, self, and identity* (pp. 111–132). Mahwah: Lawrence Erlbaum Associates.

Oppenheimer, L. (1991). The concept of action: A historical perspective. In L. Oppenheimer & J. Valsiner (Eds.), *The origins of action: Interdisciplinary and international perspectives* (pp. 1–35). New York: Springer-Verlag.

Overton, W. F. (1994). The arrow of time and the cycle of time: Concepts of change, cognition, and embodiment. *Psychological Inquiry, 5*, 215–237.

Overton, W. F. (1998). Developmental psychology: Philosophy, concepts, and methodology. In W. Damon (Series Ed.), R. M. Lerner (Volume Ed.), *The handbook of child psychology (5th Ed). Volume 1. Theoretical models of human development* (pp. 107–188). New York: Wiley.

Piaget, J. (1932). *The moral judgment of the child.* New York: Free Press.

Rorty, A. O. (1976). A literary postscript: Characters, persons, selves, individuals. In A. O. Rorty (Ed.), *The identities of persons* (pp. 301–323). Berkeley: University of California Press.

Salmivalli, C. (1999). Participant role approach to school bullying: Implications for interventions. *Journal of Adolescence, 22,* 453–459.

Salmivalli, C., Lagerspetz, K. M. J., Bjüorkqvist, K., Österman, K., & Kaukiainen, A. (1996). Bullying as a group process: Participant roles and their relations to social status within the class. *Aggressive Behavior, 22,* 1–15.

Shusterman, R. (1994). Interpretation, mind, and embodiment. *Psychological Inquiry, 5,* 256–259.

Sokol, B. W., & Chandler, M. J. (2004). A bridge too far: On the relations between moral and secular reasoning. In J. I. M. Carpendale & U. Müller (Eds.), *Social interaction and the development of knowledge* (pp. 155–174). Mahwah, NJ: Lawrence Erlbaum.

Sutton, J., & Smith, P. K. (1999). Bullying as a group process: An adaptation of the participant role approach. *Aggressive Behavior, 25,* 97–111.

Taylor, C. (1985). *Human agency and language: Philosophical papers 1.* Cambridge: Cambridge University Press.

Turiel, E., & Davidson, P. (1986). Heterogeneity, inconsistency, and asynchrony in the development of cognitive structures. In I. Levin (Ed.), *Stage and structure: Reopening the debate* (pp. 106–143). Norwood, NJ: Ablex.

Turiel, E., Hildebrandt, C., & Wainryb, C. (1991). Judging social issues: Difficulties, inconsistencies, and consistencies. *Monographs of the Society for Research in Child Development*, **56** (2, Serial No. 224).

Wainryb, C. (1991). Understanding differences in moral judgments: The role of informational assumptions. *Child Development*, **62**, 840–851.

Wainryb, C. (1993). The application of moral judgments to other cultures: Relativism and universality. *Child Development*, **64**, 924–933.

Wainryb, C. (2000). Values and truths: The making and judging of moral decisions. In M. Laupa (Ed.), *New directions for child development: Vol. 89. Rights and wrongs: How children evaluate the world* (pp. 33–46). San Francisco: Jossey-Bass.

Wainryb, C., & Turiel, E. (1993). Conceptual and informational features in moral decision making. *Educational Psychologist*, **28**, 205–218.

Wainryb, C., & Turiel, E. (1994). Dominance, subordination, and concepts of personal entitlements in cultural contexts. *Child Development*, **65**, 1701–1722.

Wiley, N. (1994). *The semiotic self*. Cambridge: Blackwell.

CONTRIBUTORS

Cecilia Wainryb (Ph.D., 1989, University of California, Berkeley) is Associate Professor of Developmental Psychology at the University of Utah. Her research interests include social and moral development, and the roles of interpretation and culture in development.

Beverly A. Brehl (M.Sc., 2004, University of Utah) is a Doctoral Candidate in Developmental Psychology at the University of Utah. She is interested in children's social cognition and moral development. Her current research concerns the role of children's developing psychological knowledge in moral reasoning.

Sonia Matwin (M.Sc., 2004, University of Utah) is a Doctoral Candidate in Social Psychology at the University of Utah. In addition to the subject matter of this Monograph, her research interests include attitudes and persuasion in the health context.

Bryan W. Sokol (Ph.D., University of British Columbia, Canada, 2004) is an assistant professor in the Department of Psychology at Simon Fraser University, Canada. His research interests include the study of children's conceptions of agency and the relation between epistemic development and moral reasoning.

Stuart Hammond (M.A., Université de Montréal, 2004) is currently a graduate student in the Department of Psychology at Simon Fraser University, Canada. His research interests include the development of children's understanding of objects through social interaction, and the relation between moral development and social interaction.

STATEMENT OF EDITORIAL POLICY

The *Monographs* series is devoted to publishing developmental research that generates authoritative new findings and uses these to foster fresh, better integrated, or more coherent perspectives on major developmental issues, problems, and controversies. The significance of the work in extending developmental theory and contributing definitive empirical information in support of a major conceptual advance is the most critical editorial consideration. Along with advancing knowledge on specialized topics, the series aims to enhance cross-fertilization among developmental disciplines and developmental sub fields. Therefore, clarity of the links between the specific issues under study and questions relating to general developmental processes is important. These links, as well as the manuscript as a whole, must be as clear to the general reader as to the specialist. The selection of manuscripts for editorial consideration, and the shaping of manuscripts through reviews-and-revisions, are processes dedicated to actualizing these ideals as closely as possible.

Typically *Monographs* entail programmatic large-scale investigations; sets of programmatic interlocking studies; or—in some cases—smaller studies with highly definitive and theoretically significant empirical findings. Multi-authored sets of studies that center on the same underlying question can also be appropriate; a critical requirement here is that all studies address common issues, and that the contribution arising from the set as a whole be unique, substantial, and well integrated. The needs of integration preclude having individual chapters identified by individual authors. In general, irrespective of how it may be framed, any work that is judged to significantly extend developmental thinking will be taken under editorial consideration.

To be considered, submissions should meet the editorial goals of *Monographs* and should be no briefer than a minimum of 80 pages (including references and tables). There is an upper limit of 175–200 pages. In exceptional circumstances this upper limit may be modified. (Please submit four copies.) Because a *Monograph* is inevitably lengthy and usually substantively complex, it is particularly important that the text be well organized and written in clear, precise, and literate English. Note, however, that authors from non-English-speaking countries should not be put off by this stricture. In accordance with the general aims of SRCD, this series is actively interested in promoting international exchange of developmental research. Neither membership in the Society nor affiliation with the academic discipline of psychology are relevant in considering a *Monographs* submission.

The corresponding author for any manuscript must, in the submission letter, warrant that all coauthors are in agreement with the content of the manuscript. The corresponding author also is responsible for informing all coauthors, in a timely manner, of manuscript submission, editorial decisions, reviews received, and any revisions recommended. Before publication, the corresponding author also must warrant in the submission letter that the study has been conducted according to the ethical guidelines of the Society for Research in Child Development.

Potential authors who may be unsure whether the manuscript they are planning would make an appropriate submission are invited to draft an outline of what they propose, and send it to the Editor for assessment. This mechanism, as well as a more detailed description of all editorial policies, evaluation process, and format requirements can be found at the Editorial Office web site (http://astro.temple.edu/-overton/monosrcd.html) or by contacting the Editor, Wills F. Overton, Temple University-Psychology, 1701 North 13th St. – Rm 567, Philadelphia, PA 19122-6085 (e-mail: monosrcd@temple.edu) (telephone: 1-215-204-7360).

Monographs of the Society for Research in Child Development (ISSN 0037-976X), one of two publications of Society of Research in Child Development, is published four times a year by Blackwell Publishing with offices at 350 Main St., Malden, MA 02148 USA and PO Box 1354, Garsington Rd, Oxford, OX4 2DQ, UK and PO Box 378 Carlton South, 3053 Victoria, Australia. A subscription to *Monographs of the SRCD* comes with a subscription to *Child Development* (published bimonthly).

INFORMATION FOR SUBSCRIBERS For new orders, renewals, sample copy requests, claims, changes of address and all other subscription correspondences please contact the Journals Department at your nearest Blackwell office (address details listed above). UK office phone: +44 (0) 1865-778315, Fax: +44 (0) 1865-471775, Email: customerservices@ oxon.blackwellpublishing.com; US office phone: 800-835-6770 or 781-388-8200, Fax: 781-388-8232, Email: subscrip@bos.blackwellpublishing.com; Asia office phone: +61 3 9347 0300, Fax: +61 3 9347 5001, Email: subscriptions@blackwellpublishingasia.com

INSTITUTIONAL PREMIUM RATES* FOR MONOGRAPHS OF THE SRCD/CHILD DEVELOPMENT 2005 The Americas $449, Rest of World £319. Customers in Canada should add 7% GST to The Americas price or provide evidence of entitlement to exemption. Customers in the UK and EU should add VAT at 5% or provide a VAT registration number or evidence of entitlement to exemption.

*Includes print plus premium online access to the current and all available backfiles. Print and online-only rates are also available.

BACK ISSUES Back issues are available from the publisher at the current single issue rate.

MICROFORM The journal is available on microfilm. For microfilm service, address inquiries to ProQuest Information and Learning, 300 North Zeeb Road, Ann Arbor, MI 48106-1346, USA. Bell and Howell Serials Customer Service Department: (800) 521-0600 × 2873.

ADVERTISING For advertising information, please visit the journal's website at www.blackwellpublishing.com/mono or contact the Academic and Science, Advertising Sales Coordinator, at journaladsUSA@bos.blackwellpublishing.com. 350 Main St., Malden, MA 02148. Phone: 781.388.8532, Fax: 781.338.8532.

MAILING Periodical postage paid at Boston, MA and additional offices. Mailing to rest of world by DHL Smart & Global Mail. Canadian mail is sent by Canadian publications mail agreement number 40573520. Postmaster: Send all address changes to Monographs of the Society for Research in Child Development, Blackwell Publishing Inc., Journals Subscription Department, 350 Main St., Malden, MA 02148-5018.

 Sign up to receive Blackwell *Synergy* free e-mail alerts with complete *Monographs of the SRCD* tables of contents and quick links to article abstracts from the most current issue. Simply go to www.blackwell synergy.com, select the journal from the list of journals, and click on "Sign-up" for FREE email table of contents alerts.

FORTHCOMING

Parental Support, Psychological Control, and Behavioral Control: Assessing Relevance across Time, Culture, and Method—*Brian K. Barber, Heidi E. Stolz, and Joseph A. Olsen* (SERIAL NO. 282, 2005)

CURRENT

Being Hurt and Hurting Others: Children's Narrative Accounts and Moral Judgments of Their Own Interpersonal Conflicts—*Cecilia Wainryb, Beverly A. Brehl, and Sonia Matwin* (SERIAL NO. 281, 2005)

Childhood Sexual Assault Victims: Long-Term Outcomes after Testifying in Criminal Court—*Jodi A. Quas, Gail S. Goodman, Simona Ghetti, Kristen W. Alexander, Robin Edelstein, Allison D. Redlich, Ingrid M. Cordon, and David P. H. Jones* (SERIAL NO. 280, 2005)

The Emergence of Social Cognition in Three Young Chimpanzees—*Michael Tomasello, and Malinda Carpenter* (SERIAL NO. 279, 2005)

Trajectories of Physical Aggression From Toddlerhood to Middle Childhood: Predictors, Correlates, and Outcomes—*NICHD Early Child Care Research Network* (SERIAL NO. 278, 2004)

Constraints on Conceptual Development: A Case Study of the Acquisition of Folkbiological and Folksociological Knowledge in Madagascar—*Rita Astuti, Gregg E. A. Solomon, and Susan Carey* (SERIAL NO. 277, 2004)

Origins and Early Development of Human Body Knowledge—*Virginia Slaughter and Michelle Heron in Collaboration with Linda Jenkins, and Elizabeth Tilse* (SERIAL NO. 276, 2004)

Mother-Child Conversations about Gender: Understanding the Acquisition of Essentialist Beliefs—*Susan A. Gelman, Marrianne Taylor, and Simone Nguyen* (SERIAL NO. 275, 2004)

The Development of Executive Function in Early Childhood—*Philip David Zelazo, Ulrich Müller, Douglas Frye, and Stuart Marcovitch* (SERIAL NO. 274, 2003)

Personal Persistence, Identity Development, and Suicide: A Study of Native and Non-Native North American Adolescents—*Michael J. Chandler, Christopher E. Lalonde, Bryan W. Sokol, and Darcy Hallett* (SERIAL NO. 273, 2003)

Personality and Development in Childhood: A Person-Centered Approach—*Daniel Hart, Robert Atkins, and Suzanne Fegley* (SERIAL NO. 272, 2003)

How Children and Adolescents Evaluate Gender and Racial Exclusion—*Melanie Killen, Jennie Lee-Kim, Heidi McGlothlin, and Charles Stangor* (SERIAL NO. 271, 2002)

Child Emotional Security and Interparental Conflict—*Patrick T. Davies, Gordon T. Harold, Marcie C. Goeke-Morey, and E. Mark Cummings* (SERIAL NO. 270, 2002)

The Developmental Course of Gender Differentiation: Conceptualizing, Measuring and Evaluating Constructs and Pathways—*Lynn S. Liben and Rebecca S. Bigler* (SERIAL NO. 269, 2002)

The Development of Mental Processing: Efficiency, Working Memory, and Thinking—*Andreas Demetriou, Constantinos Christou, George Spanoudis, and Maria Platsidou* (SERIAL NO. 268, 2002)

The Intentionality Model and Language Acquisition: Engagement, Effort, and the Essential Tension in Development—*Lois Bloom and Erin Tinker* (SERIAL NO. 267, 2001)

Children with Disabilities: A Longitudinal Study of Child Development and Parent Well-being—*Penny Hauser-Cram, Marji Erickson Warfield, Jack P. Shonkoff, and Marty Wyngaarden Krauss* (SERIAL NO. 266, 2001)

Rhythms of Dialogue in Infancy: Coordinated Timing in Development—*Joseph Jaffe, Beatrice Beebe, Stanley Feldstein, Cynthia L. Crown, and Michael D. Jasnow* (SERIAL NO. 265, 2001)

Early Television Viewing and Adolescent Behavior: The Recontact Study—*Daniel R. Anderson, Aletha C. Huston, Kelly Schmitt, Deborah Linebarger, and John C. Wright* (SERIAL NO. 264, 2001)

Parameters of Remembering and Forgetting in the Transition from Infancy to Early Childhood—*P. J. Bauer, J. A. Wenner, P. L. Dropik, and S. S. Wewerka* (SERIAL NO. 263, 2000)